KINGDO
Enacted,

THE FUTURE
KING IS HERE

THE THEOLOGY OF MATTHEW

Derek Morphew

Vineyard International Publishing
PO Box 53286,
Kenilworth 7745
Cape Town, South Africa
Email: vip@vineyardbi.org
Web: www.vineyardbi.org/vip

First published 2011, Vineyard International Publishing, Cape Town

Scripture quotations are from THE HOLY BIBLE, NEW INTER-
NATIONAL VERSION © 1973, 1978, 1984, International Bible
Society. Used by permission.

ISBN: 978-0-9869724-9-2

CONTENTS

PREFACE

This volume is part of a larger series on kingdom theology. It assumes knowledge of my primary work on this subject, *Breakthrough, Discovering the Kingdom.*[1] A brief introduction to that subject and how it leads to the subject matter of this volume will be helpful at this point.

By kingdom theology I refer to an approach to the primary message and mission of Jesus as *enacted, inaugurated eschatology.* This in turn forms part of the rediscovery of Jesus in the last century and this century that places him in the context of Second Temple Judaism. It can truly be said that since the discovery and translation of the literature of that period, Jesus research has been able to place Jesus in his historical context in a manner that was not possible in previous centuries. This rediscovery of Jesus is of major significance, since the way we see Jesus affects everything: the way we see God, salvation, mission, the Christian life, and the church.

A brief summary of enacted, inaugurated eschatology will suffice at this point. The simplest way to summarize it is through this diagram:

---

[1] Derek Morphew, *Breakthrough: Discovering the Kingdom,* Vineyard International Publishing, 2006 and Amazon Kindle publication.

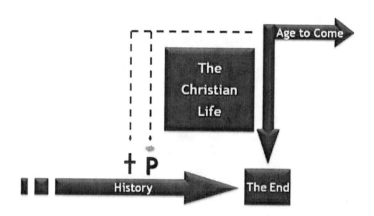

The world into which Jesus came preaching the kingdom had expectations that had grown through the centuries. These expectations were based on the coming of the kingdom in the Exodus event, the conquest of the Promised Land and the Davidic Monarchy. They were further shaped by the loss of the kingdom in the exile and the prophetic promises of Isaiah and Daniel in particular. A day would come when God would again intervene for Israel, in a final, overwhelming moment, which would terminate history as we know it and begin life at a totally new level in the Messianic age, or the age to come. The Day of Judgment would be the event that would terminate this age (the end) and usher in the coming age. From the prophetic language regarding this "end", we derive the word "eschatology" (Greek *eschatos* means "end"). The prophets spoke of the Day of the Lord, the last days, or that day.

Jesus came announcing that such a day had dawned with his arrival. Yet the way he announced and taught about the kingdom had a sense of mystery. He spoke of it as being:

- near,
- present,
- delayed, and
- future.

The only way we can bring all of this together is to understand that something mysterious, unexpected (especially to the prophets of Israel) and miraculous occurred in Jesus and the outpouring of the Spirit at Pentecost. The power of the future age broke through, from the future, into the present, setting up an altogether new dimension. Before this age has finally ended, the future age has already begun. The result is an "already" and "not yet" dimension, where the coming of the kingdom in Jesus and Pentecost is "already", but in the final sense, the coming of the kingdom is "not yet". The mysterious breakthrough of the kingdom was particularly manifest in the ministry of Jesus, as he announced it, taught about it and demonstrated it, in the cross, resurrection and ascension, and the outpouring of Pentecost. All these are demonstrations of the future breaking into the present.

Between the coming of the kingdom in Jesus ("already") and the final coming of the kingdom in Jesus ("not yet" – at his Second Coming) is the time we now live in as Christians and the church in the world. Around us is a world that lives in one dimension, in this present age, while we experience Jesus and the life in the Spirit in a new dimension, the life of the coming age, or eternal life lived now.

From this definition of the nature of the kingdom, we have developed a set of initial implications:

1. The end has come in Jesus, therefore Jesus is God.

2. The last days begin with Jesus and Pentecost, and continue

till the very end, so the whole period, from the first to the Second Coming, is the last days.

3. Every revival is a fresh in-breaking of the kingdom.

4. Every part or aspect of the kingdom is available every time it breaks through.

5. The veil torn when Jesus died shows that the separation of the present age and age to come has been torn, or opened up.

6. Therefore the powers and presence of the future age are continually available. We live in a dimension where it is always near, present, delayed and future.

7. Church history bears witness to the increasing in-breaking of the kingdom as we approach the end of the end.

8. This is the framework for understanding world missions.

9. This is the framework for understanding the Christian life, in the "already" and "not yet", making us "already – not yet" people.

10. This is the framework for understanding healing, why it occurs, yet does not always occur.

11. This is the framework for understanding the church in the world.

THREE ERAS IN GOSPEL STUDIES

There was a time when a standard requirement for students of the New Testament was to be thoroughly conversant with the intricacies of the relationship theories between Matthew, Mark and Luke, known as the "synoptic" gospels due to their similar and often overlapping content. This focus on the synoptic problem is now rather outdated. This is due to the fact that the study of the gospels has gone through three eras.

- The period when the popular approach to the gospels was *source criticism* viewed the synoptic gospels in relation to their theoretical sources, namely Matthew and Luke using Mark, Matthew and Luke using Q (Q will be explained below) and then Matthew having material of his own (M) and Luke having material of his own (L). This focus continued up to about 1950.

- The period when the popular approach to the gospels was *redaction* (or editorial) *criticism* (1950 onwards). Here the Gospel writers were viewed primarily as *theologians*.

- The most recent approach (1990's onwards) has been to view the gospels in terms of *narrative* or story. This approach is not overly concerned with issues of sources, historicity or authorship, but looks at the text itself and analysis its shape and content. Another term for this approach is "discourse analysis", which one author then further refines as "correlating culture-critical and narratological concerns."[2] The combination of the analysis of the shape of the text is combined with careful scrutiny of the social and cultural context.

Those who wish to specialize in New Testament studies will still need a detailed knowledge of the synoptic problem, but undergraduates will be unlikely to be given as much focus on this subject as was once the case.

In this work aspects of all three eras will be utilized, but the primary subject matter will be drawn from the redaction and narrative eras. Therefore, my approach will be to simply state conclusions I come to in the second half on issues of authorship, date and sources, and begin immediately to deal with the content and theology of Matthew.

My conclusions and therefore my working assumptions are as follows:

1. Matthew most probably did make use of Mark, or at least had the tradition behind Mark available to him. I rather like the idea that Peter's witness lies behind Mark, which would explain the use of Mark by Matthew and Luke.

2. Matthew and Luke share a lot of content not drawn from Mark which has been named "Q" from the German word

---

[2] For a helpful summary of these eras in relation to Lukan studies see D.A. Carson & Douglas J. Moo, *An Introduction to the New Testament,* Grand Rapids: Zondervan, 1992, (hereafter referred to as Carson & Moo), p 216–219. A typical narrative approach to the Gospels will be found in Joel Green, *The Gospel of Luke.* He says his approach "pursues a line of study to which I have referred elsewhere as 'discourse analysis' – correlating culture-critical and narratological concerns," (p 1).

for "source." It may have been a written source, or it may have been an oral tradition, or a mixture of the two.

3. Matthew has other information he has gained independently of Mark and Luke (called "M").

4. On balance, the evidence suggests to me that he wrote before the fall of Jerusalem in AD 70, but there is almost equal evidence for a date between AD 80 and AD 90.

5. While the tradition of the early church that Matthew, one of the twelve (also called Levi) was the author is problematic in some ways, there is no better available candidate. If Matthew was not the author, then we have no idea who was.

6. The most likely place of origin is either Syrian Antioch, or somewhere in Palestine.

7. In broad terms, where Mark and Luke are written with a Greco-Roman audience in mind, and are therefore more Hellenistic, Matthew shows many signs of being closer to Judaism, and is more Rabbinical in tone. John also shows more signs of the original Palestinian context, but is clearly written to counter beliefs that arose once the church had grown beyond its original Jewish context. Of the four therefore, Matthew is the most "Jewish".

THE LITERARY STRUCTURE OF MATTHEW

Beginning then with a narrative approach, we look for signs of a clear literary plan or structure. Once we have discovered Matthew's panoramic view, we can begin to delve into the content and examine more of the details.

The ending formula

Five times in Matthew a major section ends with a very similar statement:

- When Jesus had finished saying these things (7:28)
- After Jesus had finished instructing his twelve disciples (11.1)
- When Jesus had finished these parables (13.53)
- When Jesus had finished saying these things (19.1)
- When Jesus had finished saying all these things (26.1).

These ending formulae close a major section of teaching, enabling us to discover five large blocks of teaching:

- 4.23–7.28
- 7.28–10.42
- 11.1–13.52
- 13.53–18.35

• 19.1–25.46

Since these five teaching blocks make up the major central section, it becomes obvious that they are preceded and followed by two other sections: 1.1–4.22 and 26.1–28.20, giving us five sections with a prologue and epilogue, or seven major sections in all.

Then, if one looks a little closer at the five teaching blocks, it appears that there are alternating narrative (things happening) and a discourse sections (teaching). The overall structure looks like this.

1.	1.1–2.23	Prologue including Narrative	
2.	3.1–4.23	Narrative (3.1–4.23)	Discourse (5.1–7.27)
3.	7.28–10.42	Narrative (7.28–9.23)	Discourse (9.24–10.42)
4.	11.1–13.52	Narrative (11.1–12.50)	Discourse (12.51–13.52)
5.	13.53–18.35	Narrative (13.53–16.20)	Discourse (16.21–18.35)
6.	19.1–25.46	Narrative (19.1–22.46)	Discourse (23.1–25.46)
7.	26.1–28.20	Epilogue	Narrative

The alternating of narrative and discourse matches the twin aspects of the coming kingdom of God: the *works* of the kingdom and the *words* of the kingdom, or the works and words of Jesus, or demonstrating and explaining the kingdom.

The twin defining aspects of the kingdom as works and words is underlined by the fact that Matthew provides two almost identical summaries as follows:

- Jesus went throughout Galilee, *teaching* in their synagogues, *preaching* the good news of the kingdom, and *healing* every disease and sickness among the people (4.23).
- Jesus went through all the towns and villages, *teaching* in their synagogues, *preaching* the good news of the kingdom and *healing* every disease and sickness (9.35).

Notice the repeated characterization as teaching, preaching and healing (italics mine). Clearly Matthew wants us to deduce what he is saying, so he reflects it both in his literary plan and, lest we do not "get it", he twice tells us what we should deduce.

This outline raises some questions for us however, because it appears that the birth stories (prologue) and the passion narrative (epilogue) bracket the primary content (the five major blocks). Can the passion narrative be viewed as an epilogue? Surely it must be some kind of climax.

Like John

When we compare Matthew's structure to that of John, we discover that prologues and epilogues, to the Jewish literary mind, are far from mere brackets around the essential content, but the twin pillars that hold the central content in place. Here is a simple representation of John's structure.

Prologue
Ministry
    7 Signs
    7 Discourses
Cross & Resurrection
    Discourse
    Cross & resurrection
Epilogue

This can be given a bit more detail when shown as follows:

I.   The Prologue, 1: 1–18
II. Jesus' Ministry Begins, 1: 19–51
III. Signs and Public Discourses, 2: 1–12.50

1. **First Sign** – Water into wine, 2: 1–11 (interlude, 2:12)
2. Cleansing the temple, 2: 13–17
3. Destroying and raising the temple, 2: 18–22
4. Jesus and human nature, 2: 23–25
5. *First Discourse* – The new birth, 3: 1–16
6. *Second Discourse* – The water of life, 4: 1–42
7. **Second Sign** – Healing the nobleman's son, 4: 46–54
8. **Third Sign** – Healing the lame man, 5: 1–18
9. *Third Discourse* – The Divine Son, 5: 19–47
10. **Fourth Sign** – Feeding the multitude, 6: 1–15
11. **Fifth Sign** – Walking on the water, 6: 16–21
12. *Fourth Discourse* – The bread of life, 6: 22–66
13. Peter's confession, 6: 67–71
14. *Fifth Discourse* – The life-giving Spirit, 7: 1–52
15. *Sixth Discourse* – The light of the world, 8: 12–59
16. **Sixth Sign** – Healing the man born blind, 9: 1–42
17. *Seventh Discourse* – The good shepherd, 10: 1–42
18. **Seventh Sign** – The raising of Lazarus, 11: 1–57
19. The close of the public ministry, 12: 1–50

IV. The Farewell Discourses, 13: 1–17
V.   The Crucifixion, 18: 1–19: 42
VI. The Resurrection, 20: 1–29
VII. The Epilogue, 20.30–21.25 (The Purpose of the Gospel, 20:30–31)

Our purpose here is not to get distracted with John's structure, but to show two clear similarities.

First, in both Matthew and John, narrative (signs) and discourse alternate.

Second, the central section is bracketed by a prologue and epilogue-type of structure:

- The prologue in John or the birth narrative in Matthew
- The passion and resurrection narrative followed by the epilogue in John or the passion and resurrection narrative as the epilogue in Matthew.

When we study the prologue in John, we discover that it has three sections, where

- 1:1–4 summarizes chapters 1:19–6:71 (Revelation theme)
- 1:5–11 summarizes chapters 7–12 (Rejection theme) and
- 1:12–18 summarizes chapters 13–21 (Reception theme).

In this way John's prologue acts as the interpretive key to the whole book. Further, in the epilogue there is the pivotal statement of 20:30–31 which summarizes the contents of the whole Gospel. Clearly these are more than mere brackets. They are rather the pillars that hold the whole building in place.

Equally striking is the use of numbers as symbols. John uses the device of seven signs and seven discourses, because to the Jewish mind the number seven is completeness. Each discourse in John shows Jesus fulfilling one of the festivals of Israel. In Matthew, the five teaching blocks relate in some way to the five books of Moses, showing Jesus as the "greater than" Moses, but these five are part of a structure of seven parts, showing that Jesus the Messiah completely fulfils Old Testament expectations. In this way the five blocks are really the build up to the climax of the passion and resurrection "epilogue."

CLEARLY

The beginning formula

Just as pivotal are two very similar statements that appear to function as equally vital markers.

- From that time on Jesus began to preach, "Repent, for the kingdom of heaven is near" (4.17).
- From that time on Jesus began to explain to his disciples that he must go to Jerusalem and suffer many things (16.21).

These two statements divide Jesus ministry into two key aspects: his public ministry (preaching and demonstrating the kingdom) and his redemptive ministry (death and resurrection). The beginning formula of 4.17 divides what follows from what precedes it, giving us three major sections:

1. Introducing Jesus the Messiah (1.1–4.16)

2. The Ministry of Jesus the Messiah (4.17–16.20) and

3. The Journey, Suffering, Death and Resurrection of Jesus the Messiah (16.21–28.20).

Here it may be worth noticing that Matthew also likes to use the number three. We are familiar with Peter's three denials, followed by the cock crowing and how in John Jesus asks him three times, "do you love me?" In Jewish thought important matters were settled by two or three witnesses. Matthew makes use of this in many ways. There are three groups of fifteen generations in the genealogy, three temptations with three quotations, three parables against the religious authorities (21.28–22.14), three prayers of Jesus in Gethsemane, three challenges to Peter, and three denials.

The problem is, when one tries to compile this and the previous structure together, one has to somehow combine a structure of seven divisions with a structure of three divisions. This might be a problem to the contemporary Western mind, but not to Matthew, because we find there is yet a third structural aspect to Matthew.

Geographical progression

Since Matthew and Luke both seem to have used Mark, they take over Mark's fundamental outline, which gives focus to Jesus in Galilee, then on his journey to Jerusalem, and then in Jerusalem. Matthew has not only followed this outline, but he actually accentuates references to geography (e.g. 3.13; 4.12–16; 4.23–25; 9.35; 11.1; 14.13; 15.21; 15.29; 15.39; 16.13; 16.21; 17.22; 19.1; 20.17–18; 20.29; 21.1). Further, he accentuates the difference between Galilee, where Jesus had many followers, and Jerusalem, where he had many adversaries.

If one follows this geographical interest one arrives at an outline that looks like this:

1. Genealogy, Birth in Bethlehem of Judea and escape to Egypt (1.1–2.18)

2. Return to Nazareth in Galilee and preparation for ministry (2.19–4.17)

3. The Galilean ministry (4.18–15.20)

4. The ministry beyond Galilee: Tyre and Sidon (15.21–16.12)

5. Caesarea Philippi and the journey to Jerusalem (16.13–20.34)

6. The ministry in Jerusalem (21.1.1–25.46)

7. The passion and resurrection narrative (26.1–28.20)

An integrated structure

These three outlines, or structures, work somewhat independently of each other. It is not as though one fits exactly into another. Therefore, to get an overall literary plan we have to find a way to weave them into an integrated whole, knowing that Matthew does not think in terms of neat fits. The end result looks like this. The three major sections are reflected in the upper case major headings. The geographical outline is reflected in bold type, and the five blocks of teaching and narrative are reflected in italics.

PART ONE: INTRODUCING JESUS THE MESSIAH (1.1–4.16)

The Genealogy of Jesus the Messiah (1.1–1.17)

The birth of Jesus the Messiah: **Birth in Bethlehem, Escape to Egypt and return to Nazareth** (1.18–2.23)

The preparation of Jesus the Messiah: Prophetic precursor, Baptism/Anointing and Temptation (3.1–4.16)

PART TWO: THE MINISTRY OF JESUS THE MESSIAH (4.17–16.20)

The Galilean Ministry (4.17–15.20)

The *works* of Jesus (First narrative – 4.17–23)

The *words* of Jesus (First discourse – 5.1–7.27)

The *works* of Jesus (Second narrative – 7.28–9.34)

The *words* of Jesus (Second discourse – 9.35–10.42)

The *works* of Jesus (Third narrative – 11.1–12.50)

The *words* of Jesus (Third discourse – 13.1–13.52)

The *works* of Jesus (Fourth narrative – 13.53–16.20)

The ministry beyond Galilee: Tyre and Sidon (15.21–16.12)

Caesarea Philippi and the Journey to Jerusalem (16.13–20.34)

PART THREE: THE JOURNEY, SUFFERING, DEATH AND RESURRECTION OF JESUS THE MESSIAH

The *words* of Jesus (Fourth discourse – 16.21–18.35)

The *works and words* of Jesus (Fifth narrative and discourse – 19.1–25.46)

The Ministry in Jerusalem (21.1–25.46)

The death and resurrection of Jesus the Messiah (26.1–28.20)

This outline shows how the various literary divisions are not neatly set out consecutively, but run alongside one another at times. For instance the Journey begins from 16.13, but begins properly at 16.21 when Part Three is introduced.[3]

What do we get out of analyzing Matthew's literary plan? Quite a lot!

---

[3] R.T. France prefers to separate Matthew's literary plan from his "plot" assigning some aspects of his literary devices to the structure and some to the plot, *Matthew: Evangelist and Teacher,* Paternoster, 1992, p 153. He notes that the problem of running the various structures together is "particularly acute" in the case of the formula in 16.21, which falls in the middle of the account of Caesarea Philippi and Peter's confession.

The three major divisions

The three major divisions (upper case) have this logic:

1. The first section deals with the coming of the Messiah, answering the question, "who is this that comes?" The first section establishes the credentials or identity of Jesus as the Messiah. His genealogy shows him to be of Davidic descent. He is born in the city of David. His flight to Egypt and return shows that he will embody the destiny of the nation of Israel, since Israel also went into Egypt and returned to Israel. Fulfilling Old Testament Messianic expectation, he is introduced by an "Elijah like" prophet, then receives the Messianic anointing, and then in his temptations embodies Israel's journey through the wilderness. Matthew is telling us very clearly, "Here comes the Messiah."

2. The second section deals with the public ministry of the Messiah. He brings the kingdom, or better said, the kingdom breaks into history in him and through him. The in-breaking of the kingdom has two defining characteristics: works and words, demonstrating and explaining the kingdom.

3. The third section deals with the redemptive ministry of the Messiah. Further, the public ministry triggers the redemptive ministry, because the nature of his public ministry is so disturbing to the Jewish establishment that they cannot live with him. They must try to remove him.

The five blocks

The five blocks of alternating works and words tell us more.

1. The Messiah is greater than the entire Old Testament history

that precedes him. This note will become much more apparent as we delve into Matthew's details. Jesus the Messiah is "greater than" David, Solomon, the Temple, and in his five blocks of teaching, than Moses. Matthew in particular emphasizes the higher level of authority in Jesus teaching, superseding even the authority of Moses. Jesus has not come to abolish the law and the prophets, but to fulfill them (5.17). Again and again he records Jesus placing his own words above those of Moses: "You have heard that it was said to the people long ago, 'Do not murder, and anyone who murders will be subject to judgment.' But I tell you '" (5.21–22; 5.27–28; 5.33–34; 5.38–39; 5.43–44). This note, set in the first of the five blocks of teaching, climaxes in the way the first teaching section is concluded prior to the second narrative section beginning: "When Jesus had finished saying these things, the crowds were amazed at his teaching, because he taught as one who had authority, and not as their teachers of the law" (7.28–29).

2. The alternating of works and word show us that the Messiah is no mere speaker of words or doer of deeds. His deeds are explained by his words and his words are demonstrated by deeds. This is typically Jewish, or Old Testament thinking. The idea of the word of God reflected in the root word *dabar*, conveys the idea of word-events. The "word of the Lord" makes things happen. The word is itself a creative event.[4]

---

[4] For *dabar* see *The New International Dictionary of New Testament Theology, Volume III*, edited by Colin Brown, Exeter: Paternoster, p 1087–1106.

The geographical outline

The geographical outline tells us yet more.

1. Again and again Matthew links geography to Old Testament fulfillment. The Messiah had to be born in David's city (2.3–6). His journey to and from Egypt is a typological parallel to the story of Israel, which one can deduce from Jeremiah (2.17–18). The fact that his public ministry begins in Capernaum in Galilee fulfils the prophecy of Isaiah (4.12–16). There are many more details to this theme.

2. The contrast between Galilee and Jerusalem is noted repeatedly. Here geography is used to highlight two reactions to the coming of the Messiah: acceptance and rejection.

This is a fitting point to move to the next chapter. Examining Matthew's literary plan has already introduced us to his major concerns.

MATTHEW'S PRIMARY THEME

We ended the last chapter noting that Matthew emphasizes the fulfillment of Old Testament prophetic and Messianic expectation. If there is one major theme in Matthew, then perhaps this is it. From the literary plan we have learned that above all else, he is writing about the Messiah. In his three overall sections he deals with the Messianic identity, public ministry and redemptive ministry of Jesus. To say "Messiah" is to speak of one long expected and awaited in Israel. The theme of fulfillment is therefore another side of the same coin.

The way Matthew articulates the theme of fulfillment is a unique feature of his Gospel, found in what scholars have called his formula quotations, where he uses the exact same phrase again and again. There are ten that are grouped together by their almost identical language. We will note the context of each one (the almost identical language is shown in my use of italics).

The birth of Jesus

> All this took place *to fulfill what the Lord had said through the prophet*: "The virgin will be with child and will give birth to a son, and they will call him Immanuel"-- which means, "God with us" (1.22–23).

The flight to and return from Egypt

So he got up, took the child and his mother during the night and left for Egypt, where he stayed until the death of Herod. *And so was fulfilled what the Lord had said through the prophet:* "Out of Egypt I called my son" (2.14–15).

The threat from Herod

Then what was said through the prophet Jeremiah was fulfilled: "A voice is heard in Ramah, weeping and great mourning, Rachel weeping for her children and refusing to be comforted, because they are no more." So he got up, took the child and his mother during the night and left for Egypt, where he stayed until the death of Herod. (2.17–18).

His childhood in Nazareth

He went and lived in a town called Nazareth. *So was fulfilled what was said through the prophets*: "He will be called a Nazarene" (2.23).

His public ministry in Capernaum of Galilee

Leaving Nazareth, he went and lived in Capernaum, which was by the lake in the area of Zebulun and Naphtali--*to fulfill what was said through the prophet Isaiah*: "Land of Zebulun and land of Naphtali, the way to the sea, along the Jordan, Galilee of the Gentiles--the people living in darkness have seen a great light; on those living in the land of the shadow of death a light has dawned" (4.14–16).

His ministry of deliverance and healing

This was to fulfill what was spoken through the prophet Isaiah: "He took up our infirmities and carried our diseases" (8.17).

His healing ministry and the reaction of opposition from the authorities

This was to fulfill what was spoken through the prophet Isaiah: "Here is my servant whom I have chosen, the one I love, in whom I delight; I will put my Spirit on him, and he will proclaim justice to the nations. He will not quarrel or cry out; no one will hear his voice in the streets. A bruised reed he will not break, and a smoldering wick he will not snuff out, till he leads justice to victory. In his name the nations will put their hope" (12.17–21).

His use of parables as a vehicle of teaching

Jesus spoke all these things to the crowd in parables; he did not say anything to them without using a parable. *So was fulfilled what was spoken through the prophet*: "I will open my mouth in parables, I will utter things hidden since the creation of the world" (13.34–35).

Jesus entering Jerusalem on a donkey

This took place to fulfill what was spoken through the prophet: "Say to the Daughter of Zion, 'See, your king comes to you, gentle and riding on a donkey, on a colt, the foal of a donkey'" (21.4–5).

The coins of betrayal buying a potter's field

> That is why it has been called the Field of Blood to this day. *Then what was spoken by Jeremiah the prophet was fulfilled*: "They took the thirty silver coins, the price set on him by the people of Israel, and they used them to buy the potter's field, as the Lord commanded me" (27.8–10).

Further, the word or concept of fulfillment is found in other places.

- Jesus tells John that his baptism is "to fulfill all righteousness" (3.15).
- The mysterious nature of the kingdom, explained through the vehicle of parables, is described as follows: "*In them is fulfilled the prophecy of Isaiah*: 'You will be ever hearing but never understanding; you will be ever seeing but never perceiving. For this people's heart has become calloused'" (3.13–15).
- The cross, as Jesus' predicted destiny, has him telling Peter in the garden, "But how then would *the Scriptures be fulfilled* that say it must happen in this way?" (26.54).

So striking is this characteristic that many scholars have concluded that this is Matthew's primary theme.

> I remain convinced, however, that in the case of Matthew the theme I propose is one he himself would have accepted as summarizing his message, and one which has a clear content which is decisive for the whole orientation of Matthew's work. The theme I propose is that of 'fulfilment.'[5]

---

[5] R. T. France, *Matthew*, p 166, and the whole chapter, 166–205.

While this statement is perhaps technically correct, my view, as with Luke-Acts is that one cannot isolate one theme from a cluster of closely connected themes. To say "fulfillment" is to say that the Messianic era has dawned. To speak of the Messiah is to speak of someone from David's line, the anointed one, the Christ. In him the kingdom of God has come, breaking into history as inaugurated eschatology. One cannot therefore segment the theme of fulfillment from the way Matthew portrays Jesus as the embodiment of the coming kingdom. Surely one can say with equal confidence, for all the New Testament writers, that their central theme was the person: Jesus Christ. For Jesus, his primary message was the kingdom of God. All these are linked together like the strands of a single, tightly woven rope.

A sub-theme that articulates the idea of fulfillment is the "greater than" theme (my italics below). This helps us understand the way fulfillment is understood. It is not just that the whole of Old Testament expectation is fulfilled in Jesus, but the fact that it reaches its climax in him. The Messianic era more than fulfils expectations, it supersedes them. We have already noticed in the literary structure that Jesus demonstrates and teaches the kingdom in five blocks, like Moses wrote five books, but that Christ's teaching has more authority than Moses.

- The first reference to the "greater than" language is of pivotal significance, because Matthew, like Luke, shows that history itself has reached its turning point in Jesus. The age of expectation cannot be compared to the age of fulfillment. The law and the prophets were until John. Since then "the kingdom of heaven has been forcefully advancing." (11.12).

He notes the statement by Frankemülle, "This verb indicates in the briefest and most pregnant way Matthew's fundamental theological idea" p 167.

"That is why, among those born of women there has not risen anyone *greater than John the Baptist*; yet he who is least in the kingdom of heaven is greater than he" (11.11).

- I tell you that one *greater than the temple* is here (12.6).
- The men of Nineveh will stand up at the judgment with this generation and condemn it; for they repented at the preaching of Jonah, and now *one greater than Jonah* is here. The Queen of the South will rise at the judgment with this generation and condemn it; for she came from the ends of the earth to listen to Solomon's wisdom, and now *one greater than Solomon* is here. (12.41–43).
- Rather than the Messiah being the "Son of David" he is actually David's Lord (22:41–46).

In speaking of Matthew's primary themes we have therefore merged automatically into the way Matthew portrays Jesus, or what scholars call Matthew's Christology.

MATTHEW'S JESUS

Each Gospel writer elevates the person of Jesus Christ in a special way, each using their own particular language and their own way of telling the story. What is special about the way Matthew portrays Jesus?

A rather wooden way of doing this is to study the titles of Jesus in Matthew: Messiah or Christ, Son of David, Son of God, Son of Man and Lord.[6] But this method isolates the titles from the context of Matthew's story of Jesus. In terms of actual usage, what distinguishes Matthew from the other gospels is his use of the title Son of David. This is therefore a good way to get into the subject, but we will do so by combining it with a section of Matthew's actual content, namely the genealogy.

Son of David

First, let us notice the instances where Son of David is found.

- A record of the genealogy of Jesus Christ the son of David, the son of Abraham (1.1).
- An angel of the Lord appeared to him in a dream and said,

---

[6] Although he uses this approach, there is still a lot of value in Oscar Cullman, *The Christology of the New Testament,* London, SCM, 1971, particularly his treatment of the title "Son of Man."

"Joseph son of David, do not be afraid to take Mary home as your wife, because what is conceived in her is from the Holy Spirit (1.20).

- As Jesus went on from there, *two blind men* followed him, calling out, "*Have mercy* on us, Son of David!" (9.27).

- Then they brought him *a demon-possessed* man who was blind and mute, and Jesus healed him, so that he could both talk and see. All the people were astonished and said, "Could this be the Son of David?" (12.22–23).

- A Canaanite woman from that vicinity came to him, crying out, "Lord, Son of David, *have mercy* on me! My daughter is *suffering terribly from demon-possession*." (15.22).

- *Two blind men* were sitting by the roadside, and when they heard that Jesus was going by, they shouted, "Lord, Son of David, *have mercy* on us!" The crowd rebuked them and told them to be quiet, but they shouted all the louder, "Lord, Son of David, *have mercy* on us!" (20.30–32).

- They brought the donkey and the colt, placed their cloaks on them, and Jesus sat on them. A very large crowd spread their cloaks on the road, while others cut branches from the trees and spread them on the road. The crowds that went ahead of him and those that followed shouted, "Hosanna to the Son of David!" "Blessed is he who comes in the name of the Lord!" "Hosanna in the highest!" But when the chief priests and the teachers of the law saw the wonderful things he did and the children shouting in the temple area, "Hosanna to the Son of David," they were indignant (21.7–15).

- While the Pharisees were gathered together, Jesus asked them, "What do you think about the Christ? Whose son is he?" "The son of David," they replied (22.41–42).

You will notice from my italics that this title is associated with healing. It is because he is the Son of David that the people expect healing, or "mercy" of him. Those familiar with Isaiah, one of Jesus most quoted Old Testament prophets, and Matthew's most quoted prophet, will know that the Messiah of David's line will be anointed to set the captives free. When John sends messengers asking if Jesus is really "the one" (i.e. the Messiah, the Son of David), Matthew quotes Jesus reference to the defining quality of the Messiah's ministry as expected in Isaiah.

> Jesus replied, "Go back and report to John what you hear and see: The blind receive sight, the lame walk, those who have leprosy are cured, the deaf hear, the dead are raised, and the good news is preached to the poor. Blessed is the man who does not fall away on account of me" (11.4–6).[7]

For Matthew, to be Son of David is to be the liberator of human oppression, not in the narrow political expectations of Israel at the time, but in the comprehensive reversal of human oppression and suffering.

This Davidic Messiah greets one right at the start of Matthew's Gospel, in the genealogy.

The Royal Genealogy

As we examine the genealogy we discover that Matthew is not simply a recorder of Christ's genealogy, but a theologian, or more specifically a Christian skilled in the Rabbinic midrashic

---

[7] This is not a quotation of Isaiah, but an allusion, through use of classic Isaiah terminology, particularly the passage in Isaiah 61.1–2 on the year of Jubilee that Luke tells us Jesus selected for his first address to a Synagogue in Nazareth (Luke 4.16).

form of interpretation.[8] The point is not the genealogy itself, with the list of names that follow one another, but the editorial comments Matthew inserts. I have shown this by highlighting these elements.

A record of the genealogy of Jesus Christ the son of David, the son of Abraham:

> Abraham was the father of Isaac,
> Isaac the father of Jacob,
> Jacob the father of Judah *and his brothers,*
> Judah the father of Perez and Zerah, *whose mother was Tamar,*
> Perez the father of Hezron,
> Hezron the father of Ram,
> Ram the father of Amminadab,
> Amminadab the father of Nahshon,
> Nahshon the father of Salmon,
> Salmon the father of Boaz, *whose mother was Rahab,*
> Boaz the father of Obed, *whose mother was Ruth,*
> Obed the father of Jesse,
> and Jesse the father of *King* David.
> David was the father of Solomon, *whose mother had been Uriah's wife,*
> Solomon the father of Rehoboam,
> Rehoboam the father of Abijah,
> Abijah the father of Asa,

---

[8] Some, like M.D. Goulder have rather overdone how midrashic Matthew is, portraying him as all typology and midrash, so that he has no real historical interest at all. I have commented on Goulder's views in some detail in my doctoral dissertation, Derek Morphew, *A Critical Investigation of the Infancy Narratives in Matthew and Luke,* University of Cape Town, 1984.

Asa the father of Jehoshaphat,
Jehoshaphat the father of Jehoram,
Jehoram the father of Uzziah,
Uzziah the father of Jotham,
Jotham the father of Ahaz,
Ahaz the father of Hezekiah,
Hezekiah the father of Manasseh,
Manasseh the father of Amon,
Amon the father of Josiah,
and Josiah the father of Jeconiah *and his brothers at the time of the exile to Babylon.*
After the exile to Babylon:
Jeconiah was the father of Shealtiel,
Shealtiel the father of Zerubbabel,
Zerubbabel the father of Abiud,
Abiud the father of Eliakim,
Eliakim the father of Azor,
Azor the father of Zadok,
Zadok the father of Akim,
Akim the father of Eliud,
Eliud the father of Eleazar,
Eleazar the father of Matthan,
Matthan the father of Jacob,
and Jacob the father of *Joseph, the husband of Mary, of whom was born Jesus, who is called Christ.*
Thus there were fourteen generations in all from Abraham to David, fourteen from David to the exile to Babylon, and fourteen from the exile to the Christ (1.1–1.17).

1. The first thing we notice is the stated interpretation, wherein Matthew finds a double number of fourteen generations, exactly corresponding to before and after the exile.

Technically his genealogy is not accurate, because he has to leave out some links to achieve this, but "using" genealogies like this was not considered irregular amongst Jewish midrashic interpreters in his day.[9] Further, "the father of" meant equally, "the ancestor of" so one could skip generations without a problem. It so happens that in Hebrew the name David adds up to the number fourteen, which is equal to 7+7, seven being the number of completeness. Matthew is saying: "Jesus is Davidic in the most detailed manner." The whole of his ancestry, the exact number of generations show he is truly Davidic. One of his edits is "Jessie the father of *King* David." Further, as such the Messiah symbolizes, or embodies, the tragedy and hope of Israel, going into exile and coming out of exile, since in Jesus the greater return from exile has taken place. Notice also that that title "the Christ" and "Son of David" mean the same thing. David was the first and archetypal anointed one, or Christ. This subject is covered in more detail in *Breakthrough*.[10] In Psalm 2, the Messianic Psalm, Yahweh's answer to the antagonism of the nations is his King on Mount Zion (verse 6). This king is his Anointed One (Messiah/Christ – verse 2). David's ordination to this Messianic role is marked by the moment when Yahweh speaks to him saying: "You are my

---

[9] This is not the place to go into the details of exactly what Matthew has done with his sources and how freely he has edited those sources. Helpful commentaries are Dale Bruner, *Matthew: A Commentary*, Eerdmans, 2004, p 7–22; William Hendriksen, *Matthew: New Testament Commentary*, Banner of Truth, 1973, 105–129; Craig S. Keener, *A Commentary on the Gospel of Matthew*, Eerdmans, 1999, 73–80.

[10] Derek Morphew, *Breakthrough*.

Son, today I have become your Father" (verse 7). Therefore in Jewish thinking, King of Israel, Messiah and Son of God are inter-related and almost synonymous terms. But that is not all that Matthew does "theologizing" Christ's genealogy.

2. Repeatedly, in the case of Tamar, Rahab, Ruth, and Uriah's wife (Bathsheba), specific mothers are noted. This corresponds to the finale where Mary, the mother of Jesus is the final example of a mother. What is Matthew doing here? He is not simply showing that some mothers were important, or famous, just as Mary was special in God's plan. These mothers are both Gentile and involved in what we could call "shady" histories. Tamar was the daughter-in-law obliged to play the harlot in order to trick her father-in-law into keeping his promise (Genesis 38). Rahab was a Gentile harlot, Ruth was a Gentile who got under Boaz's blanket, and Uriah the Hittite was the man David had murdered to cover his sin with Bathsheba, Uriah's wife. So we have four Gentile women, whose stories included some "shady" elements. Further, the famous women normally mentioned are not there, namely Sarah, Rebekah, Rachel and Leah (the wives of Abraham, Isaac and Jacob). The primary point Matthew is making is that God uses Gentiles in the royal ancestry, so we should not be surprised when the kingdom goes out to the Gentiles. He uses sinners in his redemptive purposes, which is why the Gospel of the kingdom is "for" sinners.

3. The remaining editorial elements are "Judah *and his brothers*" and "Jeconiah *and his brothers at the time of the exile to Babylon.*" If one reads Genesis 37 the word "brothers" is

repeated a number of times, as they plot to kill Joseph. It is Judah who leads in the plot to sell him, rather than kill him. The sons of Josiah according to 1 Chronicles 3.15 were Johanan, Jehoiakim, Zedekiah and Shallum. It is not clear if Matthew intends any particular point about "brothers" here. Perhaps the point of his edit here is simply "at the time of the exile." The behavior of Judah and his brothers is not exactly noble, but sinful.

Possibly the key to Matthew's theologizing of Jesus genealogy is the comment Jesus makes when he comes to be baptized by John. A long line of confessing sinners is being baptized. John questions if it is appropriate for the Messiah to join them. Jesus says: "Let it be so now; it is proper for us to do this to fulfil all righteousness" (3.15). Jesus must identify fully with sinful humanity to redeem humanity. Where John has his famous prologue showing that the "Word became flesh", or took on full humanity, and Paul says Jesus came "in the likeness of sinful man" (Roman 8.3), Matthew shows us that way back in his ancestry, the Messiah is indentifying with sinful humanity, the whole of humanity, Israel and the Gentiles.

Matthew's Jesus is both the Messiah of Israel, truly of Israel, truly of royal descent, and also the Messiah of all of humanity, of sinful humanity.

Jesus is the Christ, the Son of David. We have looked at the latter, now a few comments on "Christ" (Messiah) in Matthew may be useful.

The Christ (Messiah)

Matthew's use of this title is not particularly different from the other synoptic writers. In his genealogy he tells us in effect that he views "Christ" as a title: "Mary, of whom was born Jesus, who is *called* Christ" – named as, entitled as, Christ (1.16). In 1.17 he uses "the Christ" again in the titular sense. From then on, when Matthew says "Jesus Christ" (1.18) we should understand that to be an abbreviated form of "Jesus the Christ", Jesus the Messiah.

Bethlehem, the city of David, is where the Christ is destined to be born (2.4). When John asks, "are you the one" it is about what "Christ" was doing. "The one" is the expected one, the Messiah (11.2).

The next occurrence links this title to another title. Peter confesses, "You are the Christ, the Son of the living God" (16.16). Then Jesus "warned his disciples not to tell anyone that he was the Christ" (16.20). Here again, Matthew's rendering of the so-called "Messianic secret" is not different from Mark or Luke. Jesus dialogue with the Pharisees about who the Christ really is, is a case of the "greater than" theme we have already alluded to (22.41–45).

Jesus warns his disciples against the worldly use of titles by those who lead them. Titles like "Rabbi" and "Father" should not be used by men. There is only one teacher in the kingdom, "the Christ" (23.10).

In the discourse about the end, Jesus warns against false Messianic pretenders (24.4–5, 23–24).

The dialogue with the High Priest in the Sanhedrin is perhaps the most instructive, both as to Matthew's understanding, and Jesus self-consciousness. Notice that once again, Christ and Son of God are viewed as almost synonymous terms, since the High Priest asks: "Are you the Christ, the Son of God" (26.63). Mark has the more Hebraic rendering, "Are you the Christ, the Son of the Blessed One" (Mark 14.61). In Mark Jesus' answer is more straightforward: "I am" Jesus said (14.62). Matthew has ""Yes, it is as you say" (26.64). Scholars who delve into the likely Aramaic phrase tend to conclude that it makes an equally affirmative statement rather like our popular "you said it!" Luke has "you are right in saying I am" (Luke 22.70). All three synoptic writers then have Jesus claiming for himself the role of the future Son of Man. As we shall see, far from being a statement about his humanity, due to its allusion to Daniel 2 and Daniel 7, this title affirms Jesus as the coming Judge of all mankind.

Pilate also refers to "Jesus who is called Christ" (27.16).

Son of God

If one follows the incidents of Son of God in Matthew the close association with Son of David and the Christ becomes apparent.

The first reference is where the devil questions if Jesus is the Son of God. This relates to the immediately preceding experience of baptism, where Jesus is anointed by the Spirit ("Christed") and hears the Father saying, "This is my Son, whom I love; with him I am well pleased" (3.17; 4.3). This statement of affirmation alludes to two well known Messianic passages, Psalm 2, where David is declared Son of God, and Isaiah 42.1 where the Servant of Yahweh is described as "my chosen one in whom I delight; I will put my Spirit on him.'" In code language therefore, at his baptism the Father ordains Jesus to the twin roles of Davidic Messiah and Suffering Servant.

Routinely in the synoptic gospels the powers of darkness acknowledge Christ's true identity while the Jewish authorities do not. The Gadarene demoniacs cry out: "What do you want with us, Son of God?" (8.29).

In response to the water-walking and storm stilling experience the disciples worshiped him, saying, "Truly you are the Son of God" (14.33).

The High Priest charges Jesus under oath: "Tell us if you are the Christ, the Son of God" (26.63). We have noted how Son of God functions here as another way of saying "Christ."

Those who mock Jesus as he hangs on the cross say: "Come down from the cross, if you are the Son of God!" (27.40 and 43). This occurs in the context of the title over his head: THIS IS JESUS, THE KING OF THE JEWS.

The Centurion, terrified by the earthquake confesses: "Surely he was the Son of God!" (27.54). This is the only case where a non-Jewish-Messianic meaning may be attached to the title.

Generally therefore, Son of God in Matthew is a title that remains within Old Testament Messianic language. It does not convey the later idea, articulated by John, of eternal Sonship or divinity, a meaning that can correctly be extended from the life of Christ, especially in post-resurrection hindsight, and which, if John is right, Jesus did have in his self-consciousness. However, the one reference that seems to echo language from the Gospel of John does take us where that Gospel takes us.

> All things have been committed to me by my Father.
> No one knows the Son except the Father, and no one
> knows the Father except the Son and those to whom
> the Son chooses to reveal him (11.27).

Three points can be made.

1. "All things" has cosmic connotations. As we shall see, this anticipates the final scene where Jesus has "all authority in heaven and on earth" (28.18).

2. The type of mutual intimate knowledge between Father

and Son, as used by John, does indicate a mutuality of divine equality. Other aspects of Matthew which we will examine later will show that he has no problem drawing such conclusions.

3. The following offer to come under Jesus yoke (11.28) probably alludes to the wisdom tradition as it had developed by the time of Jesus (possibly to Ben Sira 51.23–27). In this case the yoke offered is divine wisdom, in Matthew Jesus takes the place of divine wisdom.[11]

Our subject has edged us forward to consider the close inter-relation between Son of David, Christ, Son of God, and Son of Man. All this relates to how Jesus viewed himself. Why the "Messianic secret?" we may ask. This is where the study of isolated uses of Christological titles will not really help us. We need to inquire into how Jesus viewed himself, and how Matthew understood that, in the broader context of how Jesus understood the Messianic role, and how he came to fulfil that role. This leads us directly to the subject of the kingdom of God.

In the preface this work was introduced as a further volume in a series that articulates "enacted, inaugurated eschatology." We must ask, does that understanding of the kingdom resonate with Matthew's portrayal of "the Christ, the Son of God, the Son of David, the Son of Man"?

---

[11] R.T. France, *Matthew*, p 304. I have not addressed Matthew's use of the wisdom tradition and its application to Jesus due to the fact that it is perhaps two technical for the "level" of this publication. France's treatment of the subject is very helpful (p 302–306).

Too

Lord

As compared to Mark and Luke (who use a variety of names, like "teacher" or "master"), Matthew consistently shows the disciples addressing Jesus as Lord. He particularly avoids the use of "teacher." It seems he felt Lord, with its connotations of power and authority was the appropriate way for Jesus to be addressed. In general usage at the time, Lord was an appropriate form of address that showed polite respect. This is the minimum that Matthew indented.

However, he probably meant more than this in his use of the title. So for instance, Lord is used in contexts of Jesus return as final judge (7.21–22; 25.11, 37, 44).

> It would be going beyond the evidence to suggest that Matthew intended the use of *kurios* in relation to Jesus to be understood as a direct application of the LXX divine title *ho kurios*; but it is likely that he saw and even exploited the appropriateness of the fact that it was the same Greek word which was used for each.[12]

Enacted, Inaugurated Eschatology

These terms were defined in the preface. In *Breakthrough* more detail is provided of the way the four statements articulate New Testament thinking on the subject. The kingdom is:

- Present,
- Near,
- Delayed and
- Future.

---

[12] R. T. France, *Matthew,* p 288.

In the history of these ideas, to say that the kingdom is present is to affirm "realized eschatology", or that the kingdom is "immanent." To say that the kingdom is future is to affirm "futurist" or "apocalyptic" eschatology. To say that it is near, or delayed, is to affirm a tension between those two poles. Also in the history of New Testament scholarship is the thought that some writers are closer to realized eschatology and some closer to futurist eschatology. It is generally agreed that John, particularly with his term "eternal life" has placed greater stress on realized eschatology. Luke is said by some to have "historicized" the message of the kingdom, allowing for more of the idea that the kingdom has been delayed. The idea is that Luke as edited out some "immanent" language. This view of Luke is fairly dubious.[13] Similarly the popular view is that Mark has retained the immediacy, or immanence of the kingdom. The question is therefore, what has Matthew done with eschatology, or the manner in which the kingdom comes in Jesus the Messiah? My own view, defended in *Breakthrough,* is that all three synoptic writers included the four statements noted above, and did so because Jesus taught all four. Further, it is only through the affirmation of all four statements that one can fully grasp the mystery of the kingdom as inaugurated eschatology.

This is the real context for all the Christological titles. We therefore turn now to examine how Matthew has "edited" the tradition he received to reflect inaugurated eschatology in Jesus.

---

[13] I have commented on this in *The Mission of the Kingdom: The Theology of Luke-Acts,* Vineyard International Publishing, 2011, and Amazon Kindle publication.

The kingdom is present, near, delayed and future

One could work through Matthew's gospel tracing each of these in turn: present, then near, then delayed, then future. The disadvantage of such an approach is that it would fragment the way Jesus teaching and ministry as recorded by Matthew weaves together all four of these strands, often in the same passage.

We have already worked through Matthew's fulfillment language. Fulfillment language affirms that the long awaited Messianic era has dawned. It is here! As with Luke, this note is struck right from the infancy narrative. The Holy Spirit conceives Jesus in Mary's womb (1.18). Particularly in Isaiah's expectation, the Messianic era is a time when the Holy Spirit will be poured out in decisive finality.[14] To name Jesus "God with us" is to state a present reality (1.23). In Jesus God has visited his people. Yet we should note that even here, this name signifies that he will (future) save his people from their sins (1.21).

As with Luke, the period of Christ's infancy witnesses to a revival of prophetic phenomena. If there is one theme that connects the birth story of Jesus in Matthew it is that prophetic guidance through dreams and other means is once again occurring. This occurs after hundreds of years where the voice of the prophet had grown silent in Israel, leaving only the echo of God's voice in the scriptures. Notice the repeated reference to this phenomenon:

- An angel appeared to Joseph in a dream, telling him to respect the child born in Mary's womb (1.20).
- Wise men from the East have seen the star of the Messiah, a revelatory gift amongst the Gentiles (2.1–2).

---

[14] An appendix in *Breakthrough* details all the elements of kingdom expectation in Isaiah.

- The star moves to position itself over Bethlehem (2.9).
- They are then warned in a dream not to return to Herod (2.12).
- Then once again the angel appears to Joseph in a dream guiding him to escape to Egypt (2.13).
- After Herod dies, the angel appears once more to instruct him to return to Israel (2.19).
- Finally he is warned by the angel in a dream of the danger of Archelaus who now rules Judea, and so Joseph moves with the family to Galilee (2.22).

In the structure of the narrative each case of prophetic guidance is followed by a statement of Joseph's obedience to the angelic word, emphasizing the theme. This then is the dawn of the age of fulfillment.

Along with Mark and Luke, Matthew records the ministry of John the Baptist in eschatological terms. John comes preaching: the kingdom of heaven is "near" (3.2). Scholars have discussed this term at great length. The best illustration is that it conveys the idea of a woman in labour, shortly before the baby is born. The baby has "not yet" been born, but it is very close. We could say that "near" conveys the idea that history is pregnant with the any-minute arrival of the Messianic era.[15] Yet his message warns the people to "flee from the coming wrath" (3.7), which could convey an "end of the world" or apocalyptic moment. John's relationship to the Messiah sums up all these eschatology strands. The Messiah is he that comes (3.11 – someone who is imminent), but already now the axe is laid to the root of the trees (3.10 – judgment is now present). The Messiah's winnowing

---

[15] The various nuances of this term are explained in more detail in *Breakthrough*.

fork is already in his hand (3.12 – present) because he is about to clear his threshing floor at any moment. We will learn later how John's ministry enacts the future, eschatological ministry of Elijah, so that John is "inaugurated eschatology" personified.

At Jesus' baptism the descent of the Spirit announces that the Messiah is now present (3.16–17). One could say that this is the *moment critique* for the Messianic age to begin. At this point Jesus is formally inaugurated as the Anointed One. From now on, Israel has a resident Davidic King!

As Jesus begins his ministry his first recorded words in Matthew are: "Repent, for the kingdom of heaven is near" (4.17), conveying the same meaning of "near" as noted with the message of John.

As Jesus' ministry begins to develop, Matthew records the first of his pithy summaries:

> Jesus went throughout Galilee, teaching in their synagogues, preaching the good news of the kingdom, and healing every disease and sickness among the people (4.23).

He repeats this later on (9.35–38). The close link between the preaching or announcing of the kingdom and its demonstration or enactment in healing and deliverance shows that Isaiah's kingdom expectations are being fulfilled for all to see. A sub-set idea is that the level of authority that Jesus operates from, both in his words, which have more authority than Moses, and in his works, shows his royal or Messianic identity. In fact it suggests that the Messiah operates with the authority of God himself. This comes out clearly the first time when Jesus pronounces forgiveness over the paralyzed man in the name of the Son of Man (9.6). This anticipates a subject we will return to later. The Son of Man and Suffering Servant titles are probably the key to the way Jesus viewed himself. The Son of Man, as per Daniel 2 and 7, is an eschatological or apocalyptic figure who will determine the final destiny of mankind at the Day of Judgment (futurist eschatology), yet here we have Jesus operating in the role of the Son of Man and dispensing judgment (pardon) right now. In him the ultimate future is present.

The story of the Gadarene demoniacs presents us with the most explicit description of inaugurated eschatology. Why Matthew has two demoniacs (8.28) where Mark (5.2) and Luke have one (8.27) is not obvious. However, the words used by their "cry" are highly significant.

> "What do you want with us, Son of God?" they shouted. "Have you come here to torture us *before the appointed time*?" (italics mine).

No other Gospel writer has anything like this. The point is that while it is fairly easy to follow the four threads of Jesus teaching and trace those statements that represent the kingdom as present, near, delayed and future the critical question is, can we therefore deduce that the New Testament writers saw the kingdom of God breaking from the future into the present, or is this not an attempt to rationalize the evidence? The answer is that yes, some texts, though not many, are quite explicit. The "powers of the coming age" in Hebrews 6.5 is one. Paul describes Christians as those "upon whom the end of the ages has come" (1 Corinthians 10.11).[16] That would be another clear case. But perhaps Matthew's recording of this incident is the clearest of all, because the "appointed time" when the powers of darkness will be finally judged (i.e. at the Day of Judgment) has

---

[16] NIV translates "fulfilment" but the Greek is *telos,* the end.

now appeared "before the appointed time" in Jesus.

When the disciples of John ask why Jesus' disciples do not fast, Jesus replies that it is not appropriate to fast while the bridegroom (i.e. Jesus) is present (9.15). Any Israelite at that time would have known that the bridegroom is code language for the Messiah, in this case not only present, but embodying the Messianic banquet.[17] Here again, the ultimate future is present and available in Jesus.

As in Luke, as Jesus commissions the twelve, their message is: "the kingdom of heaven is near", carrying the same significance we have noted in the message of John and of Jesus. Yet the response or lack thereof will determine how a city stands in the "day of judgment." The kingdom is being announced now, it is very near, but the response has to do with a future apocalyptic moment. Equally significant is the tension, or nuance represented by these two statements (my italics):

> All men will hate you because of me, but he who stands firm *to the end* will be saved. When you are persecuted in one place, flee to another. I tell you the truth, you will *not finish going through the cities of Israel before the Son of Man comes* (10.22–23).

Standing firm "to the end" suggests a future, final Day of Judgment. But then the very next verse affirms that the Son of Man (a Day of Judgment figure) will come before they have completed their mission to Israel. It will occur in the near future. Luke lacks this reference in his treatment of the commission to the twelve, but makes a very similar statement elsewhere (Luke 9.27).

Jesus comments about the time when David ate the showbread:

---

[17] The appendix on Isaiah in *Breakthrough* references the Messianic banquet.

> Or haven't you read in the Law that on the Sabbath
> the priests in the temple desecrate the day and yet are
> innocent? I tell you that one greater than the temple is
> here (12.5–6).

This is an argument that does not appear at all in Mark of Luke. To state that the temple, where Yahweh is present in glory, has been superseded is a truly radical statement, one which figures in the charge of blasphemy at Jesus' trial. Notice that this presence "is here".

A comparison of Matthew and Luke's versions of the beatitudes shows that both place them in the context of the "now" and the "then" (future). For Matthew, the poor, meek etc. are blessed (now), because theirs "is" or "shall be" the kingdom, the earth, etc. Luke draws out the nuance a little more with his use of "now" and "shall."[18]

We noted above how the authority of the Son of Man exercised by Jesus has eschatological significance, since Jesus is able to administer final judgment. This note is struck again, uniquely, in Matthew's first discourse (the Sermon on the Mount). Again and again, Moses is said to have taught this or that way, yet Jesus says: "but I say to you '" (5.22, 27, 32, 34, 39, 44). In the context of Second Temple Judaism, such an elevation of authority above Moses suggests divine authority. As one "greater than" Moses Jesus embodies the presence of the kingdom beyond the most elevated expectations of the time.

Like Luke, Matthew records Jesus prayer of the kingdom. He teaches his disciples to pray: "your kingdom come" (6.10). This suggests that it still needs to come, or is an event still awaited

---

[18] The eschatological nature of the beatitudes is described in more detail in *Breakthrough*.

and longed for in some sense. Similarly the kingdom and its righteousness is something to be sought. Its presence in Jesus does not exhaust the need to pray for it and seek it (6.33). A little later Jesus warns about those who say "Lord, Lord" but may not "enter the kingdom" (7.21). Entering the kingdom is placed in the context of "that day" (7.22), namely a future moment when the final destiny of humanity will be determined. Similar futurist language occurs when Jesus comments on the faith of the centurion. Many "will come" (8.11) from East and West to the Messianic banquet, while "the subjects of the kingdom will be thrown outside, into the darkness, where there will be weeping and gnashing of teeth" (8.12). Judgment occurs at a future moment of final destiny.

Yet realized eschatology language returns when he replies to the messengers that come from John. With Luke, Matthew shows Jesus replying to them by drawing attention to what they can "hear and see" (11.2), and then deliberately alludes to kingdom expectation language from Isaiah. He then goes on to affirm that the pivotal moment of history has taken place, because the prophecy of Malachi 3.1 which expects Elijah to return to introduce Yahweh has now been fulfilled in John the Baptist (11.10). Since Jesus was introduced by John, Jesus embodies the presence of the kingdom, or the age of fulfillment, which supersedes the age of expectation (the Prophets and the Law – 11.13). The note of inaugurated eschatology is carefully stated by Matthew's tenses. John "is" the Elijah who "was to come" (11.14). "Was to come" describes the vantage point of expectation. What "was" expected "is" now present. In the transition from John to Jesus redemptive history has pivoted into the new era.

Further, the rather enigmatic statement of Jesus seems to recognize the mysterious nature of this kingdom reality: "Blessed is the man who does not fall away on account of me" (11.6). There is enough in the manner the kingdom comes in Jesus to be a cause for stumbling. Not all will be able to "accept it" (11.14). A few sentences later Matthew introduces language that one would expect in the Gospel of John, explaining that the reality that is present in Jesus requires revelation from God before it can be comprehended. "These things" have been "hidden from the wise and revealed to little children" (11.25). The intimate knowledge between the Father and the Son is known by those to whom the Son will reveal it (11.27).

It is apparent that in Jesus view, and in Matthew's portrayal of it, the coming of the kingdom is a future eschatological moment, when the Day of Judgment will take place and the final destiny of mankind will be determined. Yet again and again, this future destiny is being offered now, in the present, as Jesus announces and demonstrates the kingdom. How people respond to this present reality of the kingdom determines their future destiny in the kingdom. A case in point is the way Jesus begins to denounce Chorazin and Capernaum (11.20–24). The miracles performed in those cities should have led to an appropriate response, but their failure to respond will lead to a negative determination at the Day of Judgment.

As Jesus refutes the charges of the Pharisees in response to his liberation of the demonized, Matthew records a classic realized eschatology statement.

> But if I drive out demons by the Spirit of God, then the kingdom of God *has come upon you* (italics mine, 12.28; see also Luke 11.20).

It is no longer awaited, it is not even near, it "has come upon"[19] them as they see Jesus before their eyes demonstrating the presence of the kingdom.

In counter response, the Pharisees ask for a sign. Jesus' reply then produces terminology of the kingdom simultaneously present, near and future. Something greater than Jonah and Solomon "is here" (12.41–42), namely present in Jesus. Yet the future apocalyptic Son of Man, whose role Jesus enacts in the present, will be "in the earth" for three days and nights (12.40), an event Jesus anticipated as the climax of his ministry. Yet the destiny that is settled on the basis of those who do or do not respond to Jesus concerns the Day of Judgment (12.41–42).

The mysterious nature of the kingdom is stated once more as Jesus explains the parable of the weeds. "The knowledge of the secrets of the kingdom of heaven has been given to you" (13.11 so Luke 8.10). As those privileged to receive these secrets the disciples "see" what all previous generations of prophets and righteousness men longed to see, and never did (13.17). Here again the era of fulfillment totally supersedes the era of promise and expectation. As Craig Keener put it succinctly, "Jesus spoke in parables *because the kingdom was an end-time 'mystery' now being revealed to those with ears to hear."*[20]

We should note that Matthew quite frequently uses "kingdom" language where Mark and Luke do not. The parable of the sower in Matthew is about "the word of the kingdom" (13.19), in Mark about "the word" (Mark 4.14), and in Luke about "the word of God" (Luke 8.11).

---

[19] Few translators would now opt for "within you". It is Jesus in their midst, demonstrating the kingdom that is being referred to, not a new kind of inner awareness within the disciples.

[20] Craig Keener, *Matthew,* p 379.

 NOTE

While it is only Luke who specifically draws attention to the fact that a parable teaches the delay of the kingdom (Luke 19.11) Matthew has fairly lengthy parables unique to him that affirm the delay of the kingdom. The parable of the good seed and the weeds hardly has a parallel in Mark (4.26–29) and is absent from Luke, while in Matthew the harvest needs to be delayed to prevent the wheat being pulled up with the weeds.

> "Let both grow together until the harvest. At that time
> I will tell the harvesters: First collect the weeds and tie
> them in bundles to be burned; then gather the wheat
> and bring it into my barn" (13.30).

Then, in material unique to him (13.36–43), Matthew goes on to record Jesus explanation of this parable. Realized and future eschatology are clearly articulated here. Jesus, in the role of the Son of Man, a future apocalyptic figure, is now sowing the seed (13.37). The harvest is the end of the age (13.39, 40), when the Son of Man will play his expected role of determining the ultimate destiny of the sons of the kingdom versus sons of the evil one (13.41). Clearly therefore in Jesus a future "Son of Man" role is somehow mysteriously already at work in the present.

Matthew's parable of the net and fish makes the identical point (13.47–53).

As Jesus begins the second major part of his calling, by setting his face to Jerusalem, he begins to predict his suffering, death and resurrection. Here future and near statements are closely associated.

- "For the Son of Man is going to come in his Father's glory with his angels, and then he will reward each person according to what he has done" (16.27 – futurist language).
- "I tell you the truth, some who are standing here will not

taste death before they see the Son of Man coming in his kingdom" (16.28). This event will occur within this generation, a historically "near" moment.

The transfiguration of Jesus again introduces the role of John as personifying inaugurated eschatology. Elijah appears with Jesus in glory (17.3). The disciples therefore ask about the prediction of Malachi, that Elijah must come first to introduce Yahweh (17.10). Jesus' reply is that Elijah has come, in the person of John the Baptist, yet will still come. Notice the nuanced tenses here (my italics):

> Jesus replied, "To be sure, Elijah comes and *will restore* all things. But I tell you, Elijah *has already come,* and they did not recognize him, but have done to him everything they wished. In the same way the Son of Man is going to suffer at their hands." Then the disciples understood that he was talking to them about John the Baptist (17.11–13).

The point is not that John has replaced, or exhausted the future coming of Elijah. The point is that an event still expected at the final end has already taken place in John.

Dialogue between Jesus and his disciples on the difficulty of rich men entering the kingdom leads to further significant statements about eschatology. Two "times" are stated:

- Jesus said to them, "I tell you the truth, at the renewal of all things, when the Son of Man sits on his glorious throne, you who have followed me will also sit on twelve thrones, judging the twelve tribes of Israel.
- And everyone who has left houses or brothers or sisters or father or mother or children or fields for my sake will re-

ceive a hundred times as much and will inherit eternal life
(19.28–29).

The first statement is clearly futurist eschatology, since it concerns the renewal of all things. But those who have received
Jesus as he brings the kingdom now will receive a hundred times
reward. Here Matthew has removed the edge of clarity provided
by Mark and Luke. Mark has "now in this present age" (10.30)
and Luke has "in this age" (Luke 18.30). Both bring out more
clearly the demarcation of two ages, this age and the age to
come. By implication Jesus is operating within this age but pro-
viding the realities of the coming age. Then in the future, he will
embody the coming age. Perhaps Matthew has assumed that
the reader will understand that family members and property
describes the realities of this age.

As Jesus enters Jerusalem on a donkey he fulfills the prophecy
of Zechariah 9.9. He is the Messianic king, coming to Zion, the
people of God (21.4–9). The special feature of Matthew's version of the story is that he raises the question of Jesus identity.

> When Jesus entered Jerusalem, the whole city was
> stirred and asked, "Who is this?" The crowds answered,
> "This is Jesus, the prophet from Nazareth in Galilee"
> (21.10–11).

Such acts should prompt such questions, but as the readers we
already know the so-called Messianic secret, confessed by Peter,
that Jesus is more than a prophet, in fact more than Israel expected of a Messiah.

Once in Jerusalem Jesus conflict with the Jewish leaders in-
tensifies. His teaching becomes more confrontational towards
them. Here Matthew records that Jesus told three parables that
all concerned the status of Israel as a nation facing imminent

judgment. The sequence in Matthew is quite striking.

- First there is the word of judgment Jesus speaks on the fig tree (21.18–19 – a symbol of Israel, a nation that should have been bearing fruit).
- Then there is the parable of the two sons (21.28–31).
- The there is the parable of the landowner who planted a Vineyard and eventually sent his only Son to the tenants, after they had attacked all his previous messengers (21.33–43). The Pharisees totally "get" that Jesus is speaking about them.
- Then there is the parable of the king who gave a banquet for his son's wedding (22.1–14).

Notice here that Jesus speaks of how "The king was enraged. He sent his army and destroyed those murderers and burned their city" (22.7). This is one of various texts where Jesus predicts the destruction of Jerusalem, and event that occurred within that generation (eschatologically "near"). Yet in the same context he describes the doom that befalls one of the guests: "Tie him hand and foot, and throw him outside, into the darkness, where there will be weeping and gnashing of teeth" (22.13). Such language is normally associated with the final Day of Judgment (futurist eschatology).

It would take too long to attempt to address many of the complex issues of eschatology raised by the Mount of Olives discourse, where Jesus predicts the destruction of the temple. A few comments will be in order. First notice that the question asked by the disciples is: "When will this happen, and what will be the sign of your coming and of the end of the age?" (24.3). With hindsight we know the temple was destroyed in AD 70 (within that generation). In the preceding section Jesus says that the judgment will come upon "this generation" (23.36). Yet the disciples question is about his future coming (presumably as the Son of Man) and the end of the age. As Jesus describes the sequence of events, he tells them: "this generation will certainly not pass away until all these things have happened" (23.34). Present and ultimate futurist eschatology all seem to be woven together somehow. Then after describing the final glorious coming of the Son of Man (24.30–31) he tells various parables to illustrate his teaching. The first few emphasize any-minute readiness (Noah's flood – the thief who comes unexpectedly – 24.27–44), but the next three speak of the delay of the kingdom:

- The unfaithful servant caught out by the delay of the householder's coming (24.45–51, 48)
- The wise and foolish virgins, where the latter are caught out by the delay of the bridegroom (25.1–13)
- The nobleman who gives talents to his servants and then goes on a "journey" (25.14–30). "After a long time the master of those servants returned and settled accounts with them" (25.19).

Somehow in the mystery of the kingdom it is:

- Present in Jesus, enacted through his ministry of teaching and demonstration,
- Near, that is within this generation,
- Delayed by a long time, and
- The ultimate "end of the world" destiny of humanity.

The link between the present reality and the future coming of the kingdom is again revealed at the last supper. Jesus offers them the bread and wine (26.26–28), but will not drink it again "until that day when I drink it anew with you in my Father's kingdom" (26.29). A future Messianic banquet is present in advance in the last supper.

Finally it is Matthew in particular who describes the apocalyptic signs that occur in connection with Jesus crucifixion and resurrection. Like the others, he tells of the eclipse of the sun. Then he adds that an earthquake caused the tearing of the temple veil (27.51) and the disturbance of the graves around Jerusalem (26.52–53). Throughout scripture, such events are the labour pains of the Day of Judgment (28.2). Somehow in Jesus death and resurrection ultimate realities of the end of the world have taken place. This too is inaugurated eschatology.

Conclusion

Our examination has shown that Matthew clearly represents Jesus in terms of enacted, inaugurated eschatology.

Son of Man and Suffering Servant

There is considerable scholarly literature on the Son of Man.[21] Here all we can do is outline some of the main features and then pick up Matthew's particular record of how Jesus used this title. A trajectory of the subject begins with Daniel, follows inter-testamental literature that was influenced by Daniel, then traces the idea through the gospel writers and finally examines Paul's use of the New Adam typology. Here are some of the fundamentals.

1. Son of Man, in Hebrew thought, is simply to speak of a human being, since "son of" normally simply affirms what a person is. So we could speak of "the man", or "a man."

---

[21] My treatment of the subject will be found in *Breakthrough*, and in *The One and Only*, forthcoming Amazon Kindle publication.

2. In Aramaic *BarNarsha* (Daniel was written partly in Aramaic) reflects the same, "Bar" meaning son of, as in "Simon Bar Joseph."

3. In Hebrew the term is *BenAdam*, "Ben" meaning "Son of" as in many Hebrew surnames (BenGurion).

4. Adam, the first man, is viewed throughout scripture as one single person, and also humanity, or the first crucial representation of humanity. He is both the first man (singular) and mankind.

5. The Son of Man in Daniel is placed in the context of final judgment. In both Daniel 2 and Daniel 7 the kingdoms of this world are judged, destroyed and replaced by the kingdom of God. This event is not gradual, but cataclysmic, as the image of human kingdoms is pulverized and blown away.

6. In Daniel 7 the one who brings this final judgment is the Son of Man. The Son of Man is brought to the Ancient of Days "on the clouds of heaven" (verse 13), indicating some sort of divine or heavenly origin. He is "the man" (singular) but seems to be synonymous with "the saints of the most high." The future kingdom of God is given to the Son of Man, and to the saints of the most high (Daniel 7.14, 27) as the same recipient.

7. A concept familiar within Jewish thought, but not always understood in our culture is that of corporate personality. The destiny of mankind (the many) was found in the disastrous acts of the one man, Adam (Romans 5.12–21). Hebrews argues that later descendents (Levi) were "in" their patriarchs (Abraham – Hebrews 7.10).

8. The "man" revealed in Daniel therefore describes an individual, of heavenly origin, who contains within himself a new people of God, the saints of the most high. He brings within him a new humanity. That is why Jesus could say, "I, when I am lifted up from the earth, will draw all men to myself" (John 12.32).

9. Paul expounds this idea by showing that all of mankind is "in" either the first Adam/man, or the last Adam/man.

10. As the passage in Daniel was developed between the Testaments the idea of this heavenly "man" bringing judgment, and determining the destiny of the many, evolved. The Son of Man was seen by some as a Messianic figure.

11. However, the idea was somewhat mysterious and complex. The title did not have exact clarity within Second Temple Judaism.

12. Many passages in the gospels show that Jesus was unwilling to take conventional Messianic titles to himself in public. When Peter confessed him as the Christ, he told his disciples to tell no one. The most likely reason is not that Jesus wanted to repudiate the elevated sense of identity that such titles represented, but that he knew what they popularly meant and what popular Messianic expectations were like. He did not want to allow himself to be defined by such expectations. He therefore avoided these titles in public and deliberately reinterpreted the Messianic role. To do this the rather enigmatic Son of Man was ideal. While others called him the Christ, the Son of David and the Son of God, his favourite self-designation was the Son of Man.

13. Son of Man as a concept (corporate personality) is similar

to the other self-designation Jesus made use of, namely the Suffering Servant in Isaiah. If one examines all the passages where this figure appears in Isaiah, it sometimes refers to Israel as the servant of Yahweh, sometimes to the true remnant within Israel, and sometimes as an individual figure who embodies the destiny of the nation.[22]

14. Probably in Jesus own thinking, but certainly in Matthew's thinking, Jesus reenacts the history of Israel in his own story. The struggles, pain, hopes and future of Israel as the people of God is reenacted in and through Jesus. Son of Man and Suffering Servant are the primary "titles" that articulate this.

With these sweeping summaries of a large subject we can now examine how Son of Man is used in Matthew.

The key idea in Daniel is eschatological and relates to the final judgment of humanity. We should notice the same basic idea in Matthew. The cluster of terms and phrases used in the key texts explains the Son of Man idea rather well (accentuated text is mine)

The apocalyptic Son of Man

When the Son of Man *comes* in his glory, and all the angels with him, he will sit on his throne in heavenly glory. All the nations will be gathered before him, and he will separate the people one from another as a shepherd separates the sheep from the goats. He will put the sheep on his right and the goats on his left. Then the King will say to those on his right, "Come, you

---

[22] Dealt with in more detail in *Breakthrough*, and *The One and Only*, forthcoming Amazon Kindle publication.

who are blessed by my Father; take your inheritance, the kingdom prepared for you since the creation of the world" (25.31–34).

This sums up the idea of the Son of Man as the one who determines the destiny of humanity at judgment day. The same idea is expressed in the following examples.

As the weeds are pulled up and burned in the fire, so it will be at the end of the age. The Son of Man will send out his angels, and they will weed out of <u>his kingdom</u> everything that causes sin and all who do evil. They will throw them into the fiery furnace, where there will be weeping and gnashing of teeth (14.40–42).

For as lightning that comes from the east is visible even in the west, so will be *the coming* of the Son of Man. Wherever there is a carcass, there the vultures will gather (24.27–28).

At that time the sign of the Son of Man *will appear* in the sky, and all the nations of the earth will mourn. They will see the Son of Man *coming* on the clouds of the sky, with power and great glory. And he will send his angels with a loud trumpet call, and they will gather his elect from the four winds, from one end of the heavens to the other (24.30–31).

The following passage conveys the idea in Daniel of the sudden, cataclysmic coming of the Day of Judgment.

As it was in the days of Noah, so it will be at the *coming* of the Son of Man. For in the days before the flood, people were eating and drinking, marrying and giving in marriage, up to the day Noah entered the ark; and

they knew nothing about what would happen until the
flood came and took them all away. That is how it will
be at the *coming* of the Son of Man. Two men will be
in the field; one will be taken and the other left. Two
women will be grinding with a hand mill; one will be
taken and the other left (24.37–41).

The next two passages clearly speak of the final day of destiny,
but add factors relating to the disciples of Jesus in their relation
to the Son of Man.

For the Son of Man is going *to come* in his Father's glory
with his angels, and then he will reward each person according to what he has done. I tell you the truth, some
who are standing here will not taste death before they
see the Son of Man *coming* in his kingdom (17.27–28).

I tell you the truth, at the renewal of all things, when
the Son of Man sits on his glorious throne, you who
have followed me will also sit on *twelve thrones*, judging
the twelve tribes of Israel (19.28).

It is not surprising therefore that the High Priest understood
the exalted claim Jesus makes in his reply. Notice the explicit
allusion to the passage in Daniel by the reference to the "clouds
of heaven."

"Yes, it is as you say," Jesus replied. "But I say to all of
you: In the future you will see the Son of Man sitting
at the right hand of the Mighty One and *coming* on the
clouds of heaven" (26.64).

In all these texts, the Son of Man is said to "come" or "appear"
(my italics). Here too the figure in Daniel is being alluded to.
Apocalyptic, meaning "unveiling", refers to the belief that the

final end of history will be a moment of supreme intervention by God as judge. The Son of Man is the vehicle of this final intervention.

We should also notice the Messianic, or kingdom language associated with the Son of Man (my underlined text). Clearly by the time of Jesus, the Son of Man and the Messiah had somehow merged.

At the other end of the spectrum are texts where Jesus could as well have said "I". It is almost as though, having taken this name for himself, Jesus is more accustomed to speak of himself in the third person in this way than to say "I". Where Mark reads: Who do people say I am?" (8.27), Matthew reads,

> When Jesus came to the region of Caesarea Philippi, he asked his disciples, "Who do people say the Son of Man is?" (16.13).

In a sense one could place all the passages where Jesus predicts his death into this category, since he is predicting his personal destiny.

> The Son of Man is going to be betrayed into the hands of men. They will kill him, and on the third day he will be raised to life (17.22).

> Then a teacher of the law came to him and said, "Teacher, I will follow you wherever you go." Jesus replied, "Foxes have holes and birds of the air have nests, but the Son of Man has no place to lay his head" (8.19–20).

Jesus' present ministry

Here and now, Jesus exercises the ministry of the Son of Man. Therefore the future apocalyptic meaning casts its shadow backwards into the meaning of these cases.

> The one who sowed the good seed is the Son of Man (13.37).

> Which is easier: to say, "Your sins are forgiven," or to say, "Get up and walk"? But so that you may know that the Son of Man has authority on earth to forgive sins. … Then he said to the paralytic, "Get up, take your mat and go home" (9.5–6).

Jesus carrying the destiny of humanity in death and resurrection

In these cases the term Son of Man has intermingled with the Suffering Servant. Where the Son of Man in Daniel is a figure who exercises Divine Judgment and the Suffering Servant in Isaiah is a figure who suffers vicariously on behalf of the nation, both are figures that incorporate the many into the one. It is not surprising therefore that Jesus saw his primary identity as the Son of Man playing the role of Suffering Servant before he is revealed in the role of final Judge. The two affirmations of the Father at his baptism clearly guided him in this direction. From that day Jesus knew that his final role as ultimate Judge would come about through suffering. Once he had suffered as the representative of humanity he would judge that same humanity. In the texts below, the specifics of suffering can be deduced from the Servant passages in Isaiah, but Jesus now incorporates this into the destiny of the Son of Man, so that the former was "written" about the latter (26.23–24).

> For as Jonah was three days and three nights in the belly of a huge fish, so the Son of Man will be three days and

three nights in the heart of the earth (12.40).

Don't tell anyone what you have seen, until the Son of Man has been raised from the dead. (17.9)

In the same way the Son of Man is going to suffer at their hands. (17.12)

The Son of Man is going to be betrayed into the hands of men. They will kill him, and on the third day he will be raised to life. (17.22).

We are going up to Jerusalem, and the Son of Man will be betrayed to the chief priests and the teachers of the law. They will condemn him to death and will turn him over to the Gentiles to be mocked and flogged and crucified. On the third day he will be raised to life! (20.18–19)

As you know, the Passover is two days away--and the Son of Man will be handed over to be crucified (26.2)

Jesus replied, "The one who has dipped his hand into the bowl with me will betray me. The Son of Man will go just as it is written about him. But woe to that man who betrays the Son of Man! It would be better for him if he had not been born" (26.23–24).

Then he returned to the disciples and said to them, "Are you still sleeping and resting? Look, the hour is near, and the Son of Man is betrayed into the hands of sinners" (26.45).

All these find the clearest explanation when Jesus describes his essential calling.

> Instead, whoever wants to become great among you
> must be your *servant*, and whoever wants to be first
> must be your *slave*--just as the Son of Man did not
> come to be served, but *to serve*, and to give his life as *a
> ransom for many* (20.26–27).

Notice here that Suffering Servant terminology (serve, servant, slave, ransom for many – my italics) explains the role of the Son of Man.

Summary

Here then is the self-designation Jesus chose. He completely reinterpreted the Messianic expectations of Second Temple Judaism. His identity is both more humble than their expectations and more exalted than their expectations. Further, this identity is able to hold future eschatology (Jesus as coming Judge), Jesus present ministry in words and works, and his imminent redemptive suffering together in one overarching identity.

This is then the obvious place to track the other self-designation he chose.

The Suffering Servant

Enough has been said concerning the link between the voice of the Father at his baptism and the Servant figure in Isaiah (3.15 with Isaiah 42.1). The Father repeated this link during Jesus' transfiguration (17.5). It is worth noting that the one other gospel account where Jesus is said to have heard the Father's voice records his reference to the idea of corporate personality (John 12.30, 32). Clearly these texts convey the idea that the Father's commission to Jesus was unambiguous.

Two of Matthew's formula quotations link Christ's ministry

of healing and deliverance to the Servant passages (8.16–17; 12.15–20).

As noted above, Jesus "mission statement" confirms that he had merged the Son of Man with the Suffering Servant (20.26–27).

All these factors then explain his language at the last supper: "This is my blood of the covenant, which is *poured out for many for the forgiveness of sins*" (26.28). The words I have highlighted allude to the Servant in Isaiah (particularly 53.11–12).

The fact that Jesus was buried in the tomb of Joseph of Arimathea (27.57–60) may be a conscious association from Matthew, although one cannot be certain, it could just be a fact that he records. It would allude to Isaiah 53.9.

We could also ask, why was Jesus so clear about his forthcoming resurrection, and why did his predictions of the future destiny of the Son of Man normally speak of suffering and resurrection together? Here Isaiah 53.11–12 must have played a role: "After the suffering of his soul, he will see the light of life and be satisfied ... because he poured out his life unto death."

Jesus as Israel

Christians who have read Paul's writings will be accustomed to the idea of the church as the new Israel. What is not as well known is where this idea comes from. We have already followed the idea of corporate personality in the Son of Man and Suffering Servant identities. If one were to express the New Testament concept diagrammatically it would look like this.

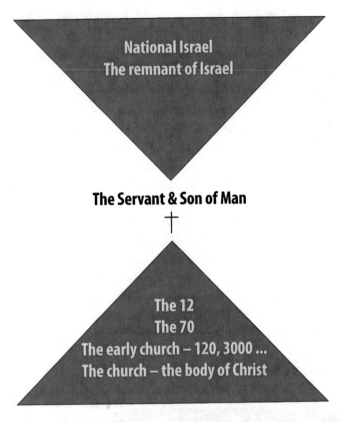

The people of God narrow down from all Israel, to the purified remnant within Israel, to the single figure of the Servant and the Son of Man, who in the case of the former embodies the suffering and judgment of the nation, and in the latter embodies the rebirth of the nation as the saints of the most high, the new humanity. This prophetic expectation is fulfilled in Jesus, who embodies the destiny of Israel within himself. He then delegates that role to the twelve, who represent the new Israel, now including both Jews and Gentiles.

Matthew does not express the full concept (one needs Paul and John to fill out the details), but he does focus on the way in which Jesus embodies the destiny of Israel.

He does this through a typically Jewish way of thinking and a particular way of reading the Old Testament. Some may call it typology, but what one means by typology then needs to be carefully defined. The essential idea is that there is a repetitive pattern in the way God brings about his redemptive purposes. Just as he once redeemed Israel from Egypt, so he will do so again in the Messianic era, but with greater glory. The Messianic era will bring the new Exodus and the true return from Babylonian exile. Read this way, many Old Testament passages that are not directly prophetic of the Messiah show through typological correspondence that they have a meaning that goes beyond what the original author intended because God is consistent in the way he does things. If you are a Jewish midrashic interpreter you can say, without embarrassment (that you are transgressing the rules of good hermeneutics) that this text "prophecies" that fulfillment, especially where Jesus re-enacts, within himself, the story of Israel.[23]

There are a number of places where Matthew makes use of this way of reading the Old Testament.

- The birth of the child called Emmanuel described in Isaiah is about a specific child to be born in the historical context of 735 BC (Isaiah 7.14), but Matthew can see a correspon-

---

[23] For an excellent description of this method of interpretation, and its use by the New Testament writers, which were all influenced by Jesus in this regard, see R. T. France, *Jesus and the Old Testament*, London: Tyndale, 1971. I have examined the subject of Midrash in some detail in Derek Morphew, *Biblical Interpretation 101*, Amazon Kindle publication, 2011.

dence with a greater child figure to be born (1.22–23).

- Isaiah spoke of the day when the Gentile nations would bring their gold and frankincense to the people of God in Zion (60.1–6). As the Magi bring their gifts they bring them to Jesus (2.10–11), the child who embodies the hopes of Israel.

- Herod's murderous actions repeat the story of Israel in Babylon (2.16–18 – Jeremiah 31.15). What happens around Jesus is actually happening to the nation of Israel "in him."

- Moses was protected from Pharaoh's murderous intentions by being hidden in a basket (Exodus 1.20–2.4), in a kind of parallel Jesus is protected in Egypt from Herod's intentions, because in all sorts of ways, he is the new and greater Moses, teaching five blocks of teaching, with greater authority, and leading the people of God in a new and greater exodus.

- Matthew quotes Hosea 11.1 in relation to Jesus returning from Egypt. The text in Hosea is about Israel, but if Jesus is "Israel personified" then his return is the nation's return.

- Moses tells Pharoah that Israel is Yahweh's first born son, therefore "Let my son go" (Exodus 4.22–23). During the wilderness journey Israel was tested by Yahweh, "as a man disciplines his son" (Deuteronomy 8.5). Therefore Jesus went into the wilderness to be tested. When the devil kept asking him "if you are the son of God" (4.1,6) Jesus replied by quoting from the same passage in Deuteronomy (4.4 citing Deuteronomy 8.3; 4.7 citing Deuteronomy 6.16; 4.10 citing Deuteronomy 6.13). He was reliving the story of Israel as the embodiment of the nation.

- In Psalm 118.22 the stone the builders rejected, which becomes the capstone, is about the vindication of Israel. Yet Jesus applies this to himself (21.42).

- Jesus alludes to Psalm 22 a number of times during his crucifixion (27.35, 39, 43, 46), but the Psalm is Israel's national lament.
- Hosea speaks of the "third day" renewal of the people of Israel (Hosea 6.2). Jesus uses this as the basis of his own "third day" resurrection (16.21; 17.23; 20.19; 21.35).

Therefore, when Jesus the Messiah dies and rises, the people of God die and rise again. His journey is their journey and their journey is his journey.

Who then is Jesus?

This is a question that Matthew is consciously prompting the reader to ask.

- If we follow the three sections of Matthew demarcated by the beginning formula: (4.17; 16.21) the ministry section ends and the journey section begins with Caesarea Philippi as the demarcating incident. This structure is associated with Mark's outline of Galilee, the journey, and then Jerusalem.
- As the ministry section draws to a close, at the end of the storm stilling incident, the disciples come to this conclusion: "Truly you are the Son of God" (14.32). It is worth noting that in Mark they ask: "Who is this? Even the wind and the waves obey him!" (Mark 4.41). Matthew has taken the question to its conclusion.
- At Caesarea Philippi Jesus confronts them with the question: "Who do people say the Son of Man is?" (16.13).
- As Jesus enters Jerusalem the crowds ask, "Who is this?" (21.10)

Clearly the major sections of Matthew's Gospel are punctuated

THE FUTURE KING IS HERE

by raising this question.

We have already noticed that the level of Christ's authority seems to show him exercising the authority of God. His words have more authority than those of Moses (5.21–22; 5.27–28; 5.33–34; 5.38–39; 5.43–44; 7.28) and his works demonstrate authority over sickness, sin, demons, death, and nature (8.9; 9.6–8; 10.1). The question of his identity is interwoven with the question of his authority. The scribes believe his claim to have the authority to forgive sins is blasphemous (9.3). This question comes to its confrontational climax once he enters Jerusalem and begins to minister in the temple. "By what authority are you doing these things?" they asked. "And who gave you this authority?" (21.23).

The level of Christ's authority, as we have already discovered, is all part of his role as the Son of Man. In playing the role of the Son of Man Jesus actually plays the role of the divine judge at the Day of Judgment. Sending out the angels to gather mankind for this moment is the prerogative of God. Here we should notice that language the Old Testament attributes to Yahweh is used for Jesus. Where in Daniel 7 the Ancient of Days sits on the throne (Daniel 7.9), in Matthew 25.31 the Son of Man sits on his throne in glory. In the parable of the weeds, the weeding out of his kingdom of "everything that causes sin and all who do evil" alludes to Zephaniah 1.3 where God is the one who will sweep away the wicked.

This merging of Jesus into the place of God goes beyond Son of Man references.

- The passage in Malachi about the eschatological role of Elijah has him introducing not the Messiah, but Yahweh himself (Malachi 4.5–6).
- As the people respond to Christ's entry into Jerusalem with

their Hosanna's, Jesus quotes Psalm 8.2, (21.16) where in fact the lips of children and infants give praise to "Yahweh, our Lord" (Psalm 8.1).

• As Jesus denounces the Jewish leaders he makes use of Isaiah 8.14 (21.42), where Yahweh is the stone they stumble on.

Matthew's climax

All this reaches its climax in the final revelation of Jesus as the risen Lord. We should notice the density of the divine allusions in this passage.

> Then the eleven disciples went to Galilee, to the mountain where Jesus had told them to go. When they saw him, they worshiped him; but some doubted. Then Jesus came to them and said, "*All* authority in heaven and on earth has been given to me. Therefore go and make disciples of *all* nations, baptizing them in the <u>name</u> of the Father and of the Son and of the Holy Spirit, and teaching them to obey *everything* I have commanded you. And surely I am with you *always*, to the very end of the age" (28.16–20).

1. The "mountain" scene recalls various theophanies of the past, particularly Moses on Mount Sinai.

2. All authority in heaven and on earth is reserved for God. So when Jesus takes this to himself, Matthew is basically affirming his divinity, although not in so many words. This gives the final meaning to the theme of authority we have already traced, particularly in his teaching (greater than Moses) and his role as the Son of Man in final judgment.

3. The "all" is enforced by the repeated used of the word.

Notice my highlights. The English text tends to mask the repetition more evident in the Greek text. The logic goes: all authority – all nations (*ethnoi* means people groups) – all his teaching – always to the end.[24] Such universal or cosmic language reinforces the point just made in 2 above.

4. This is a case of inaugurated eschatology. From Acts we have the statement that by virtue of his ascension Jesus is now "Lord and Christ" (Acts 2.36). Yet even that is preparatory, because only when he returns will all things be put under his feet and every knee will bow (1 Corinthians 15; Philippians 2). Jesus statement brings that future, ultimate authority and Lordship into the present. Now already, due to his resurrection, he *has* the authority he *will* reveal in the future. In fact, Matthew would say, from the very beginning of his ministry, in teaching and demonstrating the kingdom, Jesus *had* "all" authority.

5. The Trinitarian formula takes the attribution of divinity to Jesus a step further. We should notice that the statement is not: In the *names* of the Father, Son and Holy Spirit but in the *name* (singular) of the Father, Son and Holy Spirit. The name of God always conveys his character and attributes, particularly with the Old Testament name Yahweh.[25] This single divine character of the One God (Monotheism) is found in the Father, Son and Holy Spirit. This affirmation therefore places the three on an equal level of divinity.

6. The promise that he will be present with them to the end of the age predicates omnipresence to Jesus. This too has

---

[24] Literally "all the days."

[25] For which see *Breakthrough*, p 17–19, section on The Revelation of the Divine Name.

divine connotations.

7. It is not surprising therefore that they are said to have worshiped him. Here the term goes way beyond the idea of respect. This is the worship of the deity. R.T. France states that "some doubted" should better be translated "some were hesitant."[26] Clearly in a Jewish Monotheistic environment, to worship someone you have known and travelled with for years, whose humanity you are fully aware of, is a truly radical departure.

At the start of our analysis of Matthew's literary structure we noted that far from the infancy narrative and the passion-resurrection narratives being appendages to the structure of five blocks, they are rather like the pillars that hold the building together. Similarly in John's gospel the prologue and epilogue function as keys to the interpretation of the central series of seven discourses and signs. The way Matthew ends the gospel throws light back to the naming of Jesus: they will call him Immanuel, which means, "God with us" (1.22). Strictly speaking the name "Immanuel" could simply convey the idea that God *is* with us, as he is so often through indirect means: a prophet, king, messenger or sign. But in view of this climax, clearly Matthew means to convey that God *in person* is with us in Jesus. The whole of the gospel is therefore bracketed by the name of God. Jesus the Messiah is that name.

If the coming of the kingdom, and the person of Jesus the Messiah (King) is Matthew's central focus, and if his special way of articulating that includes the idea of fulfillment, then certain other themes equally characterize Matthew as unique or special amongst the gospels.

---

[26] R. T. France, *Matthew*, p 318, note 83.

COMMUNITY

Scholars have noted the way community functions in Matthew for some time. We will discover later that for some considerable period theories of communal authorship held the day. Most today, in the post-redaction criticism era, would think they rather overdid the evidence and failed to take note of the equally strong signs of a single, creative theological mind. Nevertheless, these scholars have rightly noted Matthew's focus on community.

What are these signs of community?

Matthew is critically conscious of three communities: the community of Israel (especially as represented by its current leadership), the community of the disciples and the community of the church that emerges from those disciples. We will examine them in their historical order.

The community of Israel

Matthew holds in tension the legitimacy of Israel as the people of Messianic expectation and the illegitimacy of the current religious system. His gospel is simultaneously the most Jewish in tone, language and content, and the most judgmental on the scribes and Pharisees. The rhetoric of Jesus condemnations has more heat in Matthew than Mark and Luke. John may come second in his negative rhetoric about "the Jews" but he does not surpass Matthew. The legitimacy side of the coin has been articulated in his fulfillment formulas. The illegitimacy aspect is widespread and frequent.

Hypocrites

Jesus repeatedly berates the Jewish leaders for their hypocrisy.

- Do not desire to be seen when you give to the poor, or when you pray, or fast, like the hypocrites do (6.2, 5, 16).
- When the Pharisees and teachers of the law questioned his disciples behavior, his reply was a scathing expose of their hypocrisy to avoid caring for their families: "Thus you nullify the word of God for the sake of your tradition. You hypocrites" (13.6–7).
- When the Herodians, in league with the Pharisees, tried to trap him in relation to the tax, his brilliant use of Caesar's image on the coin was introduced by: "You hypocrites, why are you trying to trap me?" (22.15, 18). We will notice further condemnation of their hypocrisy below.

Seven woes

While Luke has a parallel section that includes the woes of Jesus (Luke 11.39–52) Matthew has the longest section of sustained words of judgment against the Jewish religious authorities in the gospels. There is a growing tension between Jesus and these leaders, in a series of incidents, parables and teachings which culminate in the seven woes:

- The driving out of the money changers in the temple (21.12–13),

- The cursing of the fig tree (21.18–20),
- The parable of the two sons (21.28–32),
- The parable of the landowner and evil tenants (21.35–45),
- The parable of the sons banquet (21.1–14),
- The attempt of the Herodians and then the Sadducess to entrap him (22.15–33),
- The series of seven woes (23.1–37)

All this reaches its most intense moment once Jesus is in Jerusalem, teaching in the temple. He delivers a barrage of statement which climax in the repeated: "Woe to you, teachers of the law and Pharisees, you hypocrites!" (23.13, 15, 16, 23, 25, 27, 29). Their future is the place "where there will be weeping and gnashing of teeth" (24.51).

Matthew, like Mark and Luke, names the leaders of the various factions within Judaism. Sometimes he mentions the Pharisees and Sadducees (3.7), but most often he refers to the Pharisees and teachers of the law. They will certainly not enter the kingdom of heaven (5.21; 12.38; 15.1). They sit at Moses seat, but don't follow them (23.1).

Sometimes he singles out only the Pharisees (who say Jesus is demonized – 9.34; 12.2, 24; 15.12). It is particularly the Pharisees who plot to kill him (12.14), or test him, or entrap him. They are the common denominator either with the Herodians, or the Sadducees, or the Chief Priests (16.1, 5, 11; 19.3; 22.34, 41).

This generation

Another term to describe the current state of official Judaism is to speak of "this generation."

- This generation did not know how to respond to John the

Baptist, or Jesus (11.16–18).

- A wicked and adulterous generation asks for a miraculous sign! (12.39; 16.2).
- Other generations will condemn this "wicked" one at the judgment (12.40–45).
- This is an unbelieving and perverse generation (17.17).
- All the judgments of past generations will climax in the judgment on this generation (23.36).
- Jesus' predictions of the destruction of the city and the temple will be fulfilled before this generation passes away (24.34).

Following this series of confrontations the final break comes when the crowd, following its leaders, cries out for Jesus to be crucified, saying: "Let his blood be on us and on our children!"

This leads directly into the subject of Jesus predictions of destruction.

Judgment on City and Temple

Some writers give the impression that the discourse on the Mount of Olives is the only case where Jesus predicts such judgment. They construct elaborate arguments on the dating of the synoptic gospels on the basis of this discourse alone. However Matthew shows how they form part of the wider context of Jesus' radical statements about the temple. These statements were the ones, in particular, that led to his trial and crucifixion (26.61; 27.40).

Because the invited guests (Israel) rejected the King's invitation (the gospel of the kingdom offered by Jesus), the king was enraged. "He sent his army and destroyed those murderers and burned their city" (22.7). One should view the cursing of the fig tree as an acted parable of the impending destruction.

Under the current religious leaders the temple has degenerated into a den of robbers (21.12). Therefore it will be left desolate (23.38) and not one stone will be left upon another (24.1–2).

City and temple will come under judgment, within this generation!

The community of disciples

Some have described Matthew as a manual for disciples. There are in fact fairly formal notices from Matthew that most of Jesus teaching is "for" them.

- The first of the five discourses is clearly "for" the disciples: "Now when he saw the crowds, he went up on a mountainside and sat down. His disciples came to him, and he began to teach them, saying'" (5.1).
- The second discourse inserts the disciples into the formula ending, demarcating the second discourse as similarly "for" the disciples: "After Jesus had finished instructing his twelve disciples, he went on from there to teach and preach in the towns of Galilee" (11.1).
- While the third discourse begins as an address to the crowds in parables (13.1–3), it is not long before the disciples are receiving "inside" teaching on the meaning of the parables (13.10–11).
- During the fourth narrative Jesus begins to minister to the crowds through the disciples (14.15–16). Later he repeats this process (15.35).
- The fourth discourse is expressly directed to the disciples, to teach them about his destiny of redemptive suffering:

"From that time on Jesus began to explain to his disciples that he must go to Jerusalem and suffer many things at the hands of the elders, chief priests and teachers of the law, and that he must be killed and on the third day be raised to life" (16.21 also 20.17–19).

- The fifth discourse and narrative are interspersed, but as Jesus begins one of the longest blocks of teaching in that section he is said to address it "to the crowds and to his disciples" (23.1). The Olivet discourse is exclusively to the disciples (24.1).

- The end of the fifth discourse and narrative again specifies the disciples: "When Jesus had finished saying all these things, he said to his disciples, 'As you know, the Passover is two days away--and the Son of Man will be handed over to be crucified' " (26.1).

So while Jesus has a powerful ministry to the crowds, they often operate as the context for his teaching, training and equipping of the disciples.

Added to this is the deliberately private nature of many of the experiences only the disciples share with Jesus. Sometimes only Peter, James and John are present:

- The stilling of the storm (8.23–27)
- Jesus walking on the water (14.22–32)
- The encounter with the Canaanite woman (15.21–28)
- The incident at Caesarea Philippi (16.13–20) where they alone know the Messianic secret
- The transfiguration (17.1–12)
- The last supper (26.17–35)
- Gethsemane (26.36–47)
- The last climactic scene (28.16–20)

Clearly they are viewed as the inner core of the people of the kingdom of God. This is enforced by the commission to the twelve (9.37–10.4) and the fact that they come to share in his authority. All this reaches its high point in the statement made about their position in the kingdom:

> Jesus said to them, "I tell you the truth, at the renewal of all things, when the Son of Man sits on his glorious throne, you who have followed me will also sit on twelve thrones, judging the twelve tribes of Israel" (19.28).

If we were not sure that the number twelve symbolized the new people of God, then this statement settles the question.

The logic of what we have covered so far is quite self-evident.

1. The nation of Israel, especially as represented by its religious leaders, is doomed to divine judgment, within that generation. In many statements in parables, Jesus warns that the privilege of being the people of God will be taken away from them and given to others.

2. Jesus, as Son of Man, Suffering Servant and the embodiment of Israel holds the destiny of the people of God within himself. He begins a totally new departure in history, as the one in whom the future kingdom as been inaugurated in the present.

3. He gathers around him a specially chosen group of twelve leaders, who will lead the future twelve tribes, and gives most of his focus during his ministry to teaching, training and equipping them.

4. Finally he commissions them to spread the message of the kingdom to all nations.

The conclusion is obvious: a new people of God is coming into being!

Does this mean that God has rejected Israel? Who will constitute this new people?

The community of the church

Some suggest that for Matthew the church has totally replaced Israel. This is not Matthew's position, but it is certainly true that of the gospel writers, his record of Jesus words of judgment on Israel are the strongest.

Here is the crucial statement:

> I say to you that many will come from the east and the west, and will take their places at the feast with Abraham, Isaac and Jacob in the kingdom of heaven. But the subjects of the kingdom will be thrown outside, into the darkness, where there will be weeping and gnashing of teeth (8.11–12).

There are a number of points to notice here.

1. The messianic feast, particularly as anticipated by Isaiah, became almost *the* symbol of the kingdom in Second Temple Judaism, an event hosted by the famous patriarchs. Any event hosted by them has to be in essence, true Israel. This fits with other statements in Matthew which emphasize that the good news of the kingdom goes first to Israel (10.5–6; 15.24). Jesus describes "non-kingdom" behavior as typical of the Gentiles (20.24–27). In a word, it all begins with Israel.

2. But here many come from east and west while the *subjects* of the kingdom are thrown out – this is clearly a reference

to contemporary Israel.

3. The context is the incident when Jesus marvels at the faith of the Gentile Centurion. Therefore what characterizes those now included is true faith.

The idea of true Israel, added to by those of true faith, is found elsewhere. The Canaanite woman is allowed to eat the crumbs from the table of the elect because of her persistent faith (15.21–28). It is not about Israel being replaced, but Israel being redefined by true faith.

This is clarified right at the beginning by John the Baptist. Those of Jewish ethnic descent can no longer rely on their descent to guarantee their place: "And do not think you can say to yourselves, 'We have Abraham as our father.' I tell you that out of these stones God can raise up children for Abraham" (3.9). Rather, they should repent and produce the fruit of repentance.

Such faith is not only found in Gentiles who come to Jesus. Within Israel the dividing line is between the self righteous who justify themselves before God and those who willingly receive the kingdom offer of grace. Jesus came not to call the righteous, but sinners (9.13).

> I tell you the truth, the tax collectors and the prostitutes are entering the kingdom of God ahead of you. For John came to you to show you the way of righteousness, and you did not believe him, but the tax collectors and the prostitutes did. And even after you saw this, you did not repent and believe him (21.30–32).

If we ask, how can we define what faith means, then it becomes clear that true faith is defined by the nature of the response or lack of response to Jesus the Messiah. The issue with the wicked tenants was the assumption: "they will respect my son" (21.37). But they did not, in fact they killed him. That is why the landowner now gives the land to other tenants (21.41). Those who say "Lord, Lord" but fail to enter the kingdom are those who Jesus "never knew" (7.23). To know Jesus in this way is to change (repent) and become as little children (18.3). For Matthew, to know Jesus through true faith requires the fruit of obedience. In this sense Matthew stands closer to the Letter of James than many other sectors of the New Testament, where true faith shows itself by works (James 2.14–19). True faith means that one's righteousness will exceed that of the Pharisees and teachers of the law (5.20). True faith means that one cares for the hungry and thirsty members of the community as though caring for Christ (25.31–46).

What is clear is that Israel as currently constituted, with its religious leaders and their hypocrisy, cannot enter the kingdom of God. Radical change is required, compared to a resurrection.

> The manifest disintegration of the existing system is to be preliminary to the appearance of a new way of religion and a new community to embody it. And yet, it is the same temple, first destroyed, that is to be rebuilt. The new community is still Israel; there is continuity through the discontinuity. It is not a matter of replacement but of resurrection.[27]

With this foundation one can then return to the theme of the Gentiles, which we noticed in the genealogy and in the infancy narrative.

The ministry of Jesus is placed in the context of "Galilee of

---

[27] R.T. France, *Matthew*, p 227, citing C. H. Dodd in *The Founder of Christianity*, London: Collins, 1970, p 90.

the Gentiles" (4.15) or what today would be called a multicultural environment. It ends with the commission to go to all people groups (28.19). After first preaching in the towns and villages of Israel (4.23), Jesus begins to minister to people from Syria, the Decapolis and trans-Jordan (4.24). He marvels at the faith of the Gentile Centurion (8.5–13). Then just as Gentiles had visited Jesus' ministry in Galilee, so he visits the areas of Tyre and Sidon (15.21). There the Gentiles "praised the God of Israel (15.31).

The symbolic significance of the feeding of the 5000 and the 4000 (14.13–31; 15.29–31) should not be lost, one in Galilee and one on the Gentile shores of the lake of Galilee. Both Israel and the Gentiles are blessed with the miraculous bread from heaven, just as Israel was with Moses.

The mission of the kingdom will only be fulfilled when it has been preached "in the whole world as a testimony to all nations" (24.14).

The ekklesia

Matthew is the only gospel to record words of Jesus about the church (16.18; 18.17). However, we should not think of this term as we have come to think of it, looking back from Christian history, or even a reading of Acts and Paul's letters. The Greek term *ekklesia* was used to translate the Hebrew *qahal* (assembly or congregation) in the Septuagint (Greek Old Testament). It described the community of Israel as those called out (called to assemble) from the nations to be a holy people.[28] Associated terms were "elect" and "saints." This would have been the meaning in

---

[28] "Matthew's two uses of *ekklesia* do not, then, require us to believe that he knew, or even envisaged, a highly developed ecclesiastical organisation", R.T. France, *Matthew,* p 243.

the context of the ministry of Jesus. Notice that "elect" occurs a few times in the Olivet discourse (24.22, 24, 31).

Due to the age long debate between Catholic and Protestant interpretations of these texts, and the more recent discussions about their bearing on possible authorship, we should examine them a little (highlights mine).

> Simon Peter answered, "You are the Christ, the Son of the living God." Jesus replied, "Blessed are you, Simon son of Jonah, for this was not revealed to you by man, but by my Father in heaven. And I tell you that you are [Peter], and on this [rock] I will build *my church*, and the gates of Hades will not overcome it. I will give you the keys of the kingdom of heaven; whatever you bind on earth will be bound in heaven, and whatever you loose on earth will be loosed in heaven" (16.16–19) ... Jesus turned and said to Peter, "Get behind me, Satan! You are a [stumbling block] to me; you do not have in mind the things of God, but the things of men" (16.23).

> If your brother sins against you, go and show him his fault, just between the two of you. If he listens to you, you have won your brother over. But if he will not listen, take one or two others along, so that "every matter may be established by the testimony of two or three witnesses." If he refuses to listen to them, tell it to *the church*; and if he refuses to listen even to *the church*, treat him as you would a pagan or a tax collector. I tell you the truth, whatever you bind on earth will be bound in heaven, and whatever you loose on earth will be loosed in heaven. Again, I tell you that if

two of you on earth agree about anything you ask for, it will be done for you by my Father in heaven. For where two or three come together in my name, *there am I* with them (18.15–20).

1. These are the two passages where the church is mentioned (bold italics).

2. The common factor is one of authority, or to use the Rabbinical term for authority, "binding" and "loosing" (underlined). These terms have nothing to do with exorcism, as is often the way they are popularly used, or with pronouncing forgiveness (as in John 20.23), but with the exercising of authoritative teaching (making *halakhah*) which determines what behavior is appropriate or inappropriate within the community, and the opening or closing of the door of fellowship into the community of the kingdom.[29]

3. The play on words is not obvious in English. First, there is the play on words between *Petros* (Peter) and *Petra* (rock) [in brackets].[30] Second, there is the ironic interplay between Peter the "rock" who has been given the keys of the kingdom and Peter the "rock of stumbling" that he becomes a few moments later [in brackets]. The text accentuates the frail and unreliable character of the person given such authority, as in fact do many texts in Matthew that show how often the disciples had "little faith" or lacked understanding. We know too how Peter failed and denied Jesus later on.

---

[29] "These terms thus refer to a teaching function, and more specifically one of making halakhic pronouncements which are 'binding' on the people of God", R.T. France, *Matthew,* p 247.

[30] If Jesus had spoken these words in Aramaic, which he probably did.

4. In the first passage the authority is delegated to Peter (the keys). In the second passage the settling of disputes between brothers (on the basis of appropriate or inappropriate behavior) is an authority given to the church, the community.

5. The phrase "will be bound in heaven" should rather be translated "will also prove to have been bound in heaven."[31] It may be possible to argue that decisions made on earth are therefore automatically approved in heaven, which would convey quite "scary" authority given to church leaders. However, all of these statements are in the context of the inbreaking of the kingdom of God and the righteous rule of Yahweh which the twelve are authorized to announce and demonstrate. In the final commission "making disciples" is defined by the two acts of baptism and "teaching them to obey everything I have commanded you" (28.20). Key to what Jesus had commanded them was the commission to announce and demonstrate the kingdom. The announcing of the kingdom leads to the demonstration of the kingdom (10.6–8). As they say: "the kingdom of heaven is near" they heal the sick, drive out demons and raise the dead. It is authority as power to impart the presence of the eschatological future that is given to them. In that sense what they speak on earth "has been done" in heaven. They bring the rule of God in heaven into this world. While the language is Rabbinical (*torah* and *halakhah*) the meaning is now defined by the broader teaching of Jesus on the kingdom. The keys of the kingdom, to open and close the door, or bind and loose appropriate behavior, is determined by all the teaching of

---

[31] "Will be bound" and "will be loosed" has the periphrastic future perfect tense.

Jesus on the nature of the kingdom. It is charismatic (as inaugurated eschatology) rather than legal in nature.

6. The nature of the authority is determined by presence rather than precept. In both 18.20 and 28.20 the delegated authority assumes that Jesus is in the midst. Presumably therefore, if the presence of Jesus is not in the midst, what is bound on earth does not get bound in heaven. Once again the authority is charismatic rather than legal in nature.

7. Peter's individual authority should be balanced with the corporate authority of the twelve. In the first text he is given the keys of authority. In the second passage the gathered community exercises the authority. Historically, if we read Matthew with Acts in mind, Peter did open the doors of the kingdom (through announcing and demonstrating it) to Judaism (his sermon at Pentecost), to the Samaritans (with John), and to the Gentiles (Cornelius). He was the doorway to three people groups. We should notice that in each case Peter's behavior is premised on the work of the Holy Spirit, at Pentecost for obvious reasons, in Samaria because of the signs and wonders that occurred and due to the Holy Spirit coming on them through the laying on of hands, and through the way the Spirit took the initiative away from Peter at the house of Cornelius. The coming of Pentecost, as evident charismatic encounters, was the criterion of new people groups being admitted into the kingdom. The Holy Spirit actually exercised the keys of the kingdom, which Peter simply followed and cooperated with. In the second half of Acts, Paul becomes the central player, just as Peter is in the first half.[32] Further, in the church in Jerusalem Peter

---

[32] I have covered this subject in *The Mission of the Kingdom: The*

is the leader of the band of apostles as the first among equals, not as autocrat. It is Peter and John that actually open the door of fellowship to the Samaritans. His individual role is therefore balanced by corporate apostolic leadership. One can also notice that Revelation describes the heavenly city with twelve foundations, which are the twelve apostles of the lamb (21.14). In Matthew too, Jesus tells the twelve that they, and not Peter alone, will sit on twelve thrones judging the twelve tribes of Israel (20.28). Peter's authority is as representative of, and within the corporate authority of the twelve.

8. "Judging the twelve tribes" in the eschatological kingdom similarly therefore determines the meaning of the keys of binding and loosing in this context. Such language harks back to the kind of authority given to the tribal leaders and elders under Moses. The elders would "sit at the gates" of the city to judge between the people.

9. Therefore, to the extent that church leaders operate in the power of the Holy Spirit to announce and demonstrate the kingdom, follow the initiative of the Spirit in welcoming new people groups into the kingdom, and teach all that Jesus taught about the nature of the kingdom, they bring the authority of heaven to earth and utilize the keys of the kingdom. If they attempt to exercise some kind of legalistic authority where office or position is imposed on God's people without spiritual authority, they completely misconstrue Matthew's intended meaning and his reflection of Jesus commands.

Theology of Luke-Acts, Vineyard International Publishing, 2011, and Amazon Kindle publication.

10. To the extent that the church at any time emulates the legacy of the original twelve in obeying the commission of Jesus, as described above, it too exercises the keys of the kingdom. Kingdom theology therefore places Jesus teaching on the church and its delegated authority in a context that transcends the now rather worn arguments between Catholics and Protestants. These arguments have generally taken place prior to the recent rediscovery of Jesus as the eschatological Christ, or the one who brings enacted, inaugurated eschatology.

THE SYNOPTIC GOSPELS

Having examined the theology of Matthew we are now better placed to discuss the introductory issues of synoptic relationships, date, place and authorship.

Matthew, Mark and Luke have verbal or almost verbal similarities in much of their material. Their co-relationships have caused them to be described as synoptic (which means "able to be seen together") gospels. Whatever theory we adopt, we must be able to account for two things:

- striking verbal similarities (exact to almost exact wording in parallel accounts) and
- striking verbal dissimilarity (in parallel accounts).

The following example shows the striking verbal similarity between the fishers of men account found in Matthew and Mark (my italics shows the common material).

Matthew 4.18–22

As Jesus was walking beside the Sea of Galilee, he saw two brothers, *Simon* called *Peter and his brother Andrew. They were casting a net into the lake, for they were fishermen.* "Come, follow me," *Jesus said, "and I will make you fishers of men." At once they left their nets and followed him.* Going on from there, he saw two other brothers, *James son of Zebedee and his brother John. They were in a boat* with *their father Zebedee,* preparing their nets. Jesus called them, and immediately they left the boat and their father *and followed him.*

Mark 1.16–20

As Jesus walked beside the Sea of Galilee, he saw Simon and his brother Andrew casting a net into the lake, for they were fishermen. "Come, follow me," *Jesus said,* "and I will make you fishers of men." *At once they left their nets and followed him.* When he had gone a little farther, he saw *James son of Zebedee and his brother John in a boat,* preparing their nets. Without delay he called them, and they left *their father Zebedee* in the boat with the hired men *and followed him.*

Even the sections not highlighted are very similar.

The next example shows a striking verbal dissimilarity in what appear to be reports of the same teaching (highlights reflect dissimilarity).

Matthew 5.3–12

Blessed are the poor *in spirit,* for theirs is the kingdom *of heaven.*

Blessed are those who mourn, for they will be comforted.

Blessed are the meek, for they will inherit the earth'

Blessed are you when people insult you, persecute you and falsely say all kinds of evil against you because of me.

Rejoice and be glad, because great is your reward in heaven, *for in the same way they persecuted the prophets who were before you*

Luke 6.20–23

Blessed are you who are *poor*, for yours is the kingdom *of God.*

Blessed are you who hunger now, for you will be satisfied.

Blessed are you who weep now, for you will laugh.

Blessed are you when men hate you, when they exclude you and insult you and reject your name as evil, because of the Son of Man.

Rejoice *in that day and leap for joy,* because great is your reward in heaven. *For that is how their fathers treated the prophets.*

The reader immediately notices a number of verbal dissimilarities between Matthew and Luke. First, Matthew's account is longer. Second, Matthew has, "Blessed are the poor *in spirit*" rather than Luke's "the poor." One could argue that these reflect two different situations where Jesus said similar things. On the other hand, one has to explain the striking verbal similarity of the common ending they share, "'because great is your reward in heaven. For that is how their fathers treated the prophets." This would at least suggest the possibility that they were drawing on the same tradition.

Most assume that the idea that the synoptic writers drew on the same oral tradition is improbable, given the high degree of verbal agreement. There are also rare kinds of agreement: repetitions of certain Greek grammatical constructions

(Mark 2.20; Matthew 9.15) and remarkable phrases like "let the reader understand" (Matthew 24.15; Mark 13.14). There is even exact agreement in transitions. The probability that these kinds of overlaps would have occurred independently is highly improbable.

How does one explain both the similar and dissimilar chronologies if they were only drawing on memory and oral tradition? When Matthew and Luke have a narrative in common with Mark, they always agree with Mark's order, but when Mark is not the common denominator, Matthew and Luke tend to use a different order.

There are several synoptic theories. There are only two viable theories in regard to Matthew.

- The *priority of Matthew*. Perhaps Matthew wrote first, then Mark wrote using Matthew's material, then Luke wrote last using Matthew and L (an independent Lukan source). Or perhaps Matthew wrote first, then Luke, who also used L, and finally Mark.
- The *priority of Mark* has almost become "orthodoxy" because it explains more of the data. Mark wrote his gospel first. Then Matthew wrote with a copy of Mark, Q and sources only he had (M). Luke wrote with a copy of Mark, Q and sources only he had (L).

This diagram represents the probable relationships.

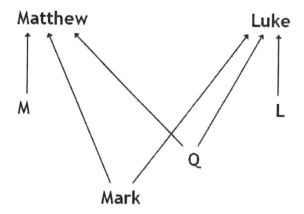

The order of events in Mark is probably earlier because wherever Matthew departs from Mark, Luke supports Mark's order. Wherever Luke departs from Mark, Matthew agrees with Mark's order. Various features indicate that Markan material reflects an earlier period (Mark's vocabulary and "feel" is more primitive).

Matthew has incorporated 51% of Mark's actual words. As a percentage of Matthew, 606 verses are from Mark, 1068 are from Q (shared with Luke) and 300 are unique to Matthew.[33]

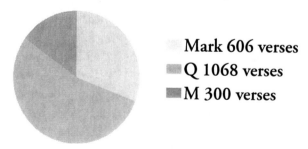

Mark 606 verses
Q 1068 verses
M 300 verses

---

[33] This data from *Harmony of the Gospels,* edited by Ralph W. Harris, Springfield: R.R. Donnelley & Sons, 1986, p 26.

As noted, when Matthew and Luke are not following Mark but have material in common, it is generally agreed that they are using a common source, namely Q. The following texts demonstrate the high probability of a Q source (my highlights of common material).

Matthew 6.28–30

> See *how the lilies* of the field *grow. They do not labor or spin. Yet I tell you that not even Solomon in all his splendor was dressed like one of these. If that is how God clothes the grass of the field, which is here today and tomorrow is thrown into the fire, will he not much more clothe you, O you of little faith?*

Luke 12.27–28

> Consider *how the lilies grow. They do not labor or spin. Yet I tell you, not even Solomon in all his splendor was dressed like one of these. If that is how God clothes the grass of the field, which is here today, and tomorrow is thrown into the fire, how much more will he clothe you, O you of little faith!*

Most suppose that this kind of agreement could only come from drawing on a common written source.

While this documentary hypothesis continues to enjoy the majority consensus amongst scholars, there is a growing tendency to question the theory.[34] The reasons and details are best left for graduate study.

---

[34] A good summary of the arguments will be found in R. T. France, *Matthew*, p 24–49. Doubts about the hypothesis are also articulated in James A. T. Robinson, *Redating the New Testament*, London: SCM, 1976.

Drawing on Oral Tradition

As moderns we are accustomed to think of documents as sources, so we assume that the kind of borrowing of sources must be the only explanation for the common features of the synoptic gospels. However, we are far removed from the way important stories were actually transmitted in the ancient near east. In some cases one notices that each writer has written the story with some freedom. Here is an example (my highlights show the common material). Notice both the common and diverging material.

Matthew 8.23–27

Then he got into the *boat* and *his disciples* followed him.

Without warning, a *furious storm* came up on the lake, so that the waves *swept over the boat*. But Jesus was *sleeping*.

The disciples went and woke him, saying, "*Lord,* save us! We're going to *drown!*"

He replied, "*You of little faith, why are you so afraid?*" Then *he got up and rebuked the winds and the waves, and it was completely calm.*

The men were amazed and asked, "What kind of man is this? Even the winds and the waves obey him!"

Mark 4.35–41

That day when evening came, he said to *his disciples,* "Let us go over to the other side." Leaving the crowd behind, they took him along, just as he was, in the *boat.* There were also other boats with him.

A *furious squall* came up, and the waves broke over the boat, so that it was nearly *swamped*. Jesus was in the stern, *sleeping* on a cushion.

The disciples woke him and said to him, "*Teacher*, don't you care if we *drown*?"

He got up, rebuked the wind and said to the waves, "Quiet! Be still!" Then the *wind died down and it was completely calm.*

He said to his disciples, "*Why are you so afraid? Do you still have no faith?*"

They were terrified and asked each other, "Who is this? Even the wind and the waves obey him!"

Luke 8.22–25

One day Jesus said to *his disciples*, "Let's go over to the other side of the lake." So they got into a *boat* and set out.

As they sailed, he fell *asleep*. A *squall* came down on the lake, so that the boat was being *swamped*, and they were in great danger.

The disciples went and woke him, saying, "Master, Master, we're going to drown!"

He got up and rebuked the wind and the raging *waters*; *the storm subsided, and all was calm.*

"*Where is your faith?*" he asked his disciples.

In fear and amazement they asked one another, "Who is this? He commands even the winds and the water, and they obey him."

Kenneth Bailey, a scholar who has spent over thirty years living among rural, Middle Eastern peasants, has given us great insight into the nature of oral culture, which is still a living tradition in that part of the world. Bailey has noted that there are three levels of control in oral tradition cultures.

1. No flexibility, as with poems and proverbs; only the exact phraseology is permitted in oral form.

2. Some flexibility, such as parables and recollections of people and events important to the identity of the community. Here there is flexibility with control. The teller is given some degree of creativity as long as all the basic story elements are there.

3. Total flexibility, such as jokes and casual news. The material is irrelevant to the identity of the community.[35]

It would seem highly probable that when the synoptic writers demonstrate some degree of creativity in their rendition of a narrative while retaining the stories' basic elements, they are following option 2. In the above example, all the elements necessary to be telling the same story are there. Jesus is in a boat with his disciples but a sudden squall comes up. So powerful is this storm that it appears that the boat will sink from the waves lapping over the sides of the boat. Jesus is asleep! The disciples wake him concerned for their welfare, amazed that Jesus could sleep through such tossing and turning. Jesus rises, rebukes them for their lack of faith and then rebukes the winds and the waves – and they go completely calm. In fear and amazement

---

[35] K. E. Bailey, "Informal Controlled Oral Tradition and the Synoptic Gospels," *Asia Journal of Theology* 5 (1991), 34–54 as referenced in Dunn, *Jesus Remembered*, 205ff.

the disciples ask, "Who is this that even the winds and waves obey him"?

Along this basic storyline the individual writers are then free, within the cultural parameters of the community, to tell the stories with some variation without destroying the essential credibility or historicity of the account. It is therefore possible that the complex relationship we explain through the borrowing of written sources may have another explanation, or more of the common features may reflect oral tradition than we imagine. Thirty years after the events people knew how a particular story went. A story showing too much creativity would be rejected as inauthentic (as was the so-called New Testament apocryphal material[36] and the Gnostic *Gospel of Thomas*). A story with all the crucial elements and just the right amount of creative license would be deemed a credible Jesus story.[37]

Conclusion

While the priority of Mark and the existence of Q as a written source remain the prevailing and most probably explanation, the entire hypothesis remains in the area of speculation. There is no hard evidence to prove it. Further, the priority of Matthew always remains a possibility. The growing understanding of oral tradition in the ancient near east may provide a totally different kind of explanation. For instance, Q may be partly a written and partly an oral source, or mostly an oral source.

---

[36] This material can be found in Wilhelm Schneemelcher, *New Testament Apocrypha*, Philadelphia: Westminster John Knox Press, 2006.

[37] James Dunn has argued extensively for this view of Gospel origins in *Jesus Remembered. Christianity in the Making: Volume I*, Michigan: Eerdmans, 2003.

AUTHORSHIP

We will first summarize the state of the debate in recent scholarship and then examine some of the details.

Recent theories

In recent scholarship, three positions have emerged concerning the authorship and origin of Matthew's gospel. There is

- The hypothesis of a community product,
- The understanding of "Matthew" as an editorial theologian (redaction criticism),
- Matthew's gospel as including an eyewitness deposit.
- The last view should be dissociated from the older, traditional belief in apostolic authorship, which is still held by some scholars.

So there are really four positions in all.

The community product

The first view was advocated by G. D. Kilpatrick.[38] He was followed by Krister Stendahl.[39] Kilpatrick advocated the view that Mark, Q and M were read in a church which developed a "targum" of these texts and finally produced a "kind of revised gospel book, conveniently incorporating into one volume the three documents of Mark, 'Q' and 'M'."[40] Stendahl, working on the Habakkuk commentary produced by the Qumran community (from whence the Dead Sea Scrolls) advocated the view that the gospel was shaped by the catechetical teaching of the early church. It was formulated as a type of training manual to be used by teachers in the community.

The editorial theologian

The first view tended to deny the individual contribution of the evangelist, and was accordingly unable to account for the strong marks of an individual and original mind which pervades the gospel. This led to a reaction in the opposite direction, and to the second view, first advocated by Bornkamm, Held and Barth.[41] The advantage of this view is that it can account for the clear evidence which is mounting as a result of the redaction-critical method. Clearly the author shaped the tradition he had received in order to present Jesus in a particular manner. The

---

[38] G. D. Kilpatrick, *The Origins of the Gospel According to Saint Matthew,* Oxford: Clarendon, 1946.

[39] Krister Stendahl, *The School of Saint Matthew and its Use of the Old Testament,* Philadelphia: Fortress, 1968.

[40] Ralph P. Martin, "St. Matthew's Gospel in Recent Study," *Expository Times,* 80, 1969, p 132.

[41] Günther Bornkamm, Heinz Joachim Held & Gerhard Barth, *Tradition and Interpretation in Matthew,* London: SCM, 1963.

author is now no longer the school, but the individual representative of a community which may have had a school. This position then goes further and emphasizes that the author was a theologian in his own right who was formulating what he believed to be the answer to a particular church situation. In this case we do not find the original tradition of Jesus in Matthew a much as an understanding of Jesus in a particular church situation.

The second view has the difficulty of neglecting the tradition received at the expense of the tradition remoulded. Both these positions, the first and the second, have the difficulty of being unable to explain the persistent tradition of the early church concerning apostolic authorship.[42] But the older view of apostolic authorship could not explain the fact than an apostolic author had based his work upon a non-apostolic writer (Mark).[43] In addition, the tradition it relied upon (the early church tradition from Papias) mentioned a Hebrew gospel whereas the present Matthew was clearly written in Greek. A view was needed which could account for both the redactional (edited) nature of Matthew's gospel and the persistent tradition of the early church. In other words, there was need of a hypothesis which could account for the initial and formative influence of an apostolic witness while at the same time accounting for the evident non-apostolic nature of the present gospel. The

---

[42] See E. Stewart Petrie, "The Authorship of 'The Gospel According to Matthew', A Reconstruction of the External Evidence," *New Testament Studies*, 14, 1967–68, p 15–30.

[43] This "problem" must assume the correctness of the two-source theory (Matthew and Luke used Mark and Q). This assumption may not be correct. See Charles H. Talbert on the "significant assault on the 'two-source theory' since 1963" in "Shifting Sands, The Recent Study of the Gospel of Luke", *Interpretation*, 30, 1976, 381–395, p 393.

need for the former requirement was made more evident by the discovery of elements in Matthew which indicated that the tension between church and synagogue was still very much alive when the tradition was first documented. These elements have been highlighted by the work of Günther Bornkamm, Gerhard Barth and Sjef van Tilborg.[44] They seem to demand a time before the church had totally lost touch with the synagogue.[45]

---

[44] Ralph P. Martin, "Recent Study", p 134; Bornkamm, Held and Barth, *Tradition and Interpretation*, Sjef van Tilborg, *The Jewish Leaders in Matthew*, Leiden: E. J. Brill, 1972. The fact that Matthew has accentuated Christ's condemnation of the Pharisees and the Jewish authorities has been evident to redaction critics for some time, e.g. T. Francis Glasson, "Anti-Pharisaism in St. Matthew", *Jewish Quarterly Review*, 51, 1961, p 316–320. The evidence of tension is discussed by Bornkamm in Bornkamm, Held and Barth, *Tradition and Interpretation*, p 20–24, 26, 31–32, 39. "Matthew's Gospel confirms throughout that the congregation which he represents had not yet separated from Judaism – the struggle with Israel is still within its walls", p 50–51; by Barth, p 71,79,81,89. On Matthew 5.23 and 17.24 he says, "Both sayings are only possible in the situation before the destruction of the Temple", p 90. On 24.20 he says, "The severe tension between Church and Judaism in Matthew's Gospel would make this addition intelligible", p 92. On 5.10–11; 10.23; 23.34 he says, "It is true that the church in Matthew seeks to keep fellowship with the Jewish nation, but the situation is tense", p 111. This evidence tends to indicate that while the church did form separate Synagogues (assemblies) from the beginning (Acts 11.26; Galatians 1.22) much as the Hellenistic Jews had done, it still attempted to remain within Israel as a nation. It was this stance, as being "within" and yet "separate" which caused the severe tension.

[45] J. A. T. Robinson, *Redating the New Testament*, London: SCM, 1976, p 103–104. The conclusions that are drawn from these signs of tension are not always the same. Van Tilborg, *The Jewish Leaders in Matthew*, makes an excellent examination of the Matthean use of "hypocrites", "evil people" and "murderers" and shows how they

reflect a deep sense of antagonism between the Jewish authorities and the Christian community in Matthew. But the conclusion he draws from his research is to say the least, surprising.

> To my mind there is one conclusion that can be drawn. Matthew lived in a world in which Judaism was no longer a serious competitor. If one wishes to call the Jews who have refused to be converted hypocrites, evil people, murders and imposters, there must be a fairly great and satisfactory distance on a historical level (p 171).

This is not logic. Human experience proves exactly the opposite. The more the sense of religious competition, the more the sense of religious antagonism, the more one will find expressions of extreme denunciation. The greater the distance in time, the less the actual threat, the more moderate the sense of disagreement will become. One could quote some lively examples from the history of the church in South Africa and the history of Apartheid.

Douglas Hare has carefully examined *The Theme of Jewish Persecution of Christians in the Gospel According to Matthew,* London: Cambridge University Press, 1967. He concludes that Matthew's gospel arose in an environment where the church had already parted company with the Jewish Synagogues and where the Pharisees were in control of the Synagogues (p 19–79). The church had become utterly pessimistic about evangelising the Jewish nation (p 146–149) because their attempts had failed (146–166). The insertion of the *Birkath ha-Minim* into the synagogue prayer after AD 75 shows that this total separation of church and synagogue only occurred after AD 70. This leads him to date the Gospel after AD 70. We must agree with Hare in his central thesis, namely that the Jewish persecution of Christians in Matthew's church and in the first century in general hardly ever led to death. We also accept his view that persecution rose in intensity during the period of the two wars (AD 69–70 and AD 135). However, his position does involve a number of problems which make his conclusions of the dating of Matthew questionable.

The insertion of the *Birkath ha-Minim* surely indicates the end

These requirements lead to the third position.

process of the split between church and synagogue. The beginning of this split must have come much earlier. One wonders in fact whether the church had not left the synagogue some time before AD 70, despite the common assumption to the contrary. The book of Acts and the Pauline letters tend to show that while Christian evangelists entered synagogues to evangelise, the Christian converts formed synagogues (assemblies) of their own right from the beginning (Acts 11.26; Galatians 1.22). Comments in Matthew about the "synagogue across the road" need not argue for a date after AD 70. Here one notices that Hare has to reject Raymond Brown's view of the exclusion of Christians from the synagogues in John's gospel (p 49, note 3).

Hare believes that persecution was worse after AD 70. In order to hold this view he has to minimise evidence of persecution before AD 70. He rejects the historicity of the accounts in Acts and he evades the importance of 1 Thessalonians 2.14–16, (p 62–63). One must also question whether Hare has correctly understood the meaning of "peace" in Acts 9.31. Does peace mean the absence of persecution?

Hare argues that persecution in the diaspora was worse than in Judea. Can this view be sustained in view of the letter to the Hebrews? Granted that it was written to a Jewish Christian group somewhere in the diaspora (possibly Rome), does it not indicate that the temptation was to slide back into Judaism at a time when persecution was now in the past rather than give in to Judaism while under the pressure of persecution? See for instance the comments made by F. F. Bruce, *Commentary on the Epistle to the Hebrews, NICNT,* Grand Rapids: Eerdmans, 1964, p xxiii–xxx, xlii–xliv, 266–270. In fact the persecution seems not to have been from Jews at all (Hebrews 10.32–34). In general this letter tends to indicate that persecution was worse in the earlier period than the later period, and that is was worse in Judea than in the diaspora.

His arguments on the pessimism of Matthew's church are the weakest part of his study. In this section (p 146–149) he gives very little evidence at all. He quotes Matthew 22.8 f and 28.19f, which need not indicate what he presumes.

It is interesting to notice in connection with Hare's views that E.

The apostolic deposit

This is sometimes called the proto-Matthew hypothesis. C. F. D. Moule advocated the view that behind the present gospel there lies a collection of "Aramaic traditions which were translated and ultimately collected, conflated and arranged together with the other material, by another scribe, a Greek writer."[46] Perhaps Matthew is the source behind the Aramaic traditions, but the gospel we have today is the product of a later Greek writer.

Robert H. Gundry has drawn his conclusions from a detailed investigation of Matthew's quotations of the Old Testament.[47] He believes that these quotations give evidence of a triple linguistic tradition, based upon Septuagintal (Greek Old Testament), Aramaic and Hebrew sources.[48] In his view, such a triple

---

L. Abel, who proposes two authors, namely Matthew 1 and Matthew 2, places the fiercely anti-pharisaic part of the gospel in the section attributed to Matthew 1, who he believes wrote before AD 70, E. L. Abel, "Who Wrote Matthew", *New Testament Studies*, 17, 1970–71, p 138–152.

[46] R. P. Martin, "Who wrote?" p 135.

[47] Robert H. Gundry, "The Language Milieu of First Century Palestine: It's Bearing on the Authenticity of the Gospel Tradition", *JBL*, 83, 1964, p 404–408.

[48] So for instance in the infancy narrative, according to Gundry, "The Language Milieu", with the direct quotations 1.23 is wholly Septuagintal (p 89–90), 2.6 agrees with both the Septuagint and the MT (Hebrew text – p 91–93), in 2.15 Matthew translates the MT independently, as he seems to have done in 2.18 (p 94–97), and most theories regarding 2.23 must assume some knowledge of Hebrew and Greek (p 97–104). As regards the allusive quotations, 1.21 is independent from the Septuagint and shows targumic influence (p 127–128), 2.1–2 is based on the Septuagint (p 128–129) as is 2.11 (p 129–130), 2.13 is an independent rendering of the Hebrew (p 130),

language phenomenon could only occur in Palestine. He then goes on to affirm the view that this Palestinian tradition emanates from the apostle Matthew.[49]

With this introduction in place, we can now examine some of the details.

The tradition of the early church

The early church is unanimous that Matthew, the apostle, was the author. However, the tradition is problematic.

Papias

The primary source for the early church tradition is Papias. Later writers also mentioned Matthew's authorship, but most believe they were all reflecting Papias's testimony. They are:

- Irenaeus: "Now Matthew published also a book of the Gospel among the Hebrews in their own dialect, while Peter and Paul were preaching the gospel in Rome and founding the Church".[50]
- Pantaenus, as cited by Eusebius, said the Gospel, written by Matthew in Hebrew, had preceded him to India.
- Origin also says Matthew composed the gospel in Hebrew.[51]

There are a number of issues that arise.

---

and 2.20–21 reflects both the Septuagint and the MT, with the latter being more prominent (p 130–131).

[49] E. L. Abel also finds that elements of the present gospel go back to an eye-witness or apostolic deposit, "Who Wrote Matthew", p 138–152.

[50] Irenaeus, *Adversus Haereses* (Against Heresies), iii.1.1, also cited in Donald Guthrie, *New Testament Introduction*, Leicester: IVP, 1990, p 47.

[51] Cited by Guthrie, p 47.

We do not have Papias's original words, only quotations of him by later writers, namely Eusebius and Irenaeus. From Eusebius one can deduce that he lived and wrote around AD 140. From Irenaeus we can deduce that he would have written around AD 110–120. The difference is that according to Irenaeus, Papias knew the apostle John, and was therefore in direct contact with the apostolic generation. The later date would prohibit that. On balance, Irenaeus is probably to be followed.[52]

His statement, via Eusebius, can be translated in a number of ways. He says:

> Matthew composed the *logia* (sayings) in the Hebrew dialect and each translated them as best he could.

The Greek text of his words is open to a number of possible translations.

- "Composed" could be compiled, or arranged.
- *Logia* according to common usage referred to the "oracles" of God, and so could refer to the whole Old Testament. In this context, it could refer to all the teachings of Jesus (i.e. not the narrative sections) or alternatively, to the words *and* works of Jesus. The latter is more probable because if one examines Papias's use of *logia* elsewhere it also refers to the whole gospel of Mark.[53] So one can take *logia* to refer to the whole gospel without straining the text.
- "Hebrew dialect" at face value refers to the Hebrew language (or perhaps Aramaic, a more common and recent Se-

[52] Due to the fact that Eusebius did not like Papias's eschatology and tended to discount his claims.

[53] D.A. Carson & Douglas J. Moo, *An Introduction to the New Testament,* Grand Rapids: Zondervan, 1992, p 145, hereafter referred to as Carson & Moo.

THE FUTURE KING IS HERE

mitic language spoken by Jesus and most Jews at the time). However, it could possible mean a Hebrew "style" or way of writing.[54] On balance, this is not an obvious way of reading the expression.

- "Translated" could mean what it usually means, but if "dialect" as style is assumed, it could mean that each "interpreted" what Matthew wrote as best he could.

Scholars can speculate on such matters at length. The problem is that if we take the most obvious meaning of Papias's words, it seems he must have been mistaken. The current gospel of Matthew can only have been written in Greek, not Hebrew. There are many reasons for this, but one which we have already dealt with is that many of his formula quotations (central to Matthew) depend upon the Septuagint (Greek Old Testament). Further, his incorporation of large sections of Mark, which was written in Greek, would be difficult to explain if he first wrote in Hebrew or Aramaic. Unless of course one wants to dispute the fact that Matthew made use of Mark.

If Papias was wrong about the language Matthew wrote in, was he right in attributing the gospel to Matthew? Of course, he may have received reliable information from the apostolic witnesses he knew that Matthew was the author, and simply made the wrong guess about the original language due to the evident Rabbinic style of the gospel.

Anonymity

A popular view among scholars is that the ascriptions: "According to Matthew, Mark," etc., were only added in the second century, around AD 125. Prior to that, they circulated without

---

[54] Carson & Moo, p 144, Guthrie, p 46.

the name of the author attached. However, more recently this assumption has been questioned. Martin Hengel, having examined the way books were distributed in the first century, and how authorship was attached to them, concludes that it would not have been possible for the gospels to circulate in the church for any length of time without an author being attached to them.

> The anonymity of the attributions in the second century cannot be explained by anything other than the assumption that the titles were part of the works from the beginning. It is inconceivable, he argues, that the gospels could circulate anonymously for up to sixty years and then in the second century suddenly display unanimous attribution to certain authors.[55]

The evidence from the early church is both unanimous and persistent. There is no other candidate from the early church other than the apostle Matthew.

Theories of evolving authorship

How can one square the unanimous witness of the early church with the features of the gospel we have today? One way of taking due note of both pieces of evidence is to conceive of the extant gospel incorporating the contribution of Matthew the apostolic author, who wrote in Hebrew, while the final author of our gospel wrote in Greek. There are a number of possibilities.

1. Matthew could have been the author of what we call Q.[56]

---

[55] Carson & Moo, p 141, citing Martin Hengel, *Studies in the Gospel of Mark*, Philadelphia: Fortress Press, 1985.
[56] Guthrie, p 45.

This theory tends to go with the idea that *logia* refers to sayings, rather than narrative, since Q has more teaching material than narrative. If Matthew the apostle wrote Q, then added what we call M to that, one would have a large section of the extant Matthew attributed to him. However, Q is a totally hypothetical document. If Matthew did write something in Hebrew, then it has vanished without a trace.

2. Another theory is that he wrote a document with the formula quotations and various "testimonia" (Old Testament texts used to show Jesus as the Messiah). Again, this document is a speculation, and there is no trace of it.

3. Some authors therefore simply speak of a Matthew 1 versus Matthew 2. The gospel we have is Matthew 2 (written in Greek, probably not by the apostle). Matthew 1, perhaps in Hebrew, was used as a source. This may have been written by Matthew the apostle. This idea gives due weight to the testimony of Papias, but does not view Matthew as the author of our current gospel.

Arguments against Matthew

Most scholars today do not accept that the author was Matthew the apostle. Here are some of their reasons:

1. Matthew used Mark. Why would an apostolic author borrow from a non-apostolic writer? This argument is counter-balanced by the early church tradition that Mark was Peter's scribe. If Peter's authority was behind Mark, then it would make sense for Matthew to use him. Further, incorporating other manuscripts was not viewed in the same way as it is in our time, with copyright problems and so on.

2. Matthew does not read like Mark, which is much more vivid and shows signs of an eye-witness. It is true that Matthew lacks the eye-witness feel of Mark, but this can be countered by the Rabbinic midrashic style of Matthew. Those steeped in Jewish ways of thinking and writing would not write in the style of an uneducated evangelist and fisherman like Peter. In the end such arguments tend to be rather subjective.

3. Matthew shows signs of a developed understanding of the church, which could only have emerged at a later date. However, this idea all depends upon how one reads the way Matthew refers to the church. We have shown above that it does not necessarily show signs of a later development of church structures.

Some clues that suggest Matthew's authorship

Where Mark and Luke use the name "Levi" for the call of Matthew (Mark 2.14; Luke 5.27), Matthew uses the name "Matthew" (9.9). In all the lists of the twelve apostles, the name Matthew appears in the list, not Levi. Could this be Matthew's subtle notice of authorship?

The attention to detail is an obvious characteristic of the gospel. A tax collector might be expected to write like this.

Matthew uses the more precise "four-drachma coin" (*nomisma*) for the payment of tribute, where Mark and Luke use the more general *dynarion* to refer to coins. A tax collector would tend to do this.

However, these are just clues. They fall short of any sort of proof of apostolic authorship.

Conclusion

With the information at our disposal at the present, it is not possible to be dogmatic about any view of Matthean authorship. What does seem to be required is,

- In some sense a recognition of the early church tradition on apostolic authorship,
- A recognition of the redactional nature of the present gospel (used Mark and Q), and
- A recognition of the Jewish-Palestinian origins of much of the material.

My own opinion is that Papias made an incorrect assumption about the original language but that the only evidence we have points to Matthew the apostle. It is of course possible that Matthew the apostle wrote Q and M in Hebrew or Aramaic, then got hold of Mark and re-wrote the present gospel in Greek, editing his first version.

DATE

Who the author was is perhaps not as important as the date of Matthew. There are two viable options, a date prior to AD 70, and a date between AD 80 and 100.

The later date

Most scholars date Matthew after the fall of Jerusalem, and therefore somewhere between AD 80 and 100.[57] Most of those who opt for the later date either do not believe that Jesus could have predicted the fall of Jerusalem in AD 70 with that amount of accuracy or, due to the fact that the language of Matthew shows knowledge of the event, believe he has edited the original words of Jesus.[58] It cannot be dated much later than AD 80–100 because both Ignatius and the *Didache* appear to cite Matthew. Other arguments for a later date are the developed understanding of the church and signs that the break with

---

[57] For instance W.G. Kümmel, *Introduction to the New Testament*, London: SCM, 1970, p 84; R.E. Nixon, "Matthew", *New Bible Commentary*, Norman Perrin, *The New Testament, an Introduction*, New York: Harcourt Brace Javonavich, 1974, p 172; Craig Keener, *A Commentary on the Gospel of Matthew*, Grand Rapids: Eerdmans, 1999, p 42–44 opts for the later seventies.

[58] For instance Matthew 22.7

the synagogue was now a thing of the past. The insertion of the *Birkat ha-Minim*[59] into the synagogue prayer after AD 75 shows that this total separation of church and synagogue only occurred after AD 70.[60] Matthew highlights Jesus opposition to the Pharisees more than Mark or Luke. The Pharisees became more of an issue for the church in Syria-Palestine after AD 70.[61] Matthew reflects a worldview closer to the rabbis than the other gospels, but the rabbis rose to prominence in Judaism after AD 70.[62] Comments in Matthew about how things are "until today" (11.12; 27.8; 28.15) must assume a later historical era. Generally these scholars believe Matthew reflects some considerable theological reflection, particularly his high Christology, which indicates a later date. It does not seem to show any knowledge of Paul's letters, which must have begun to circulate by the late part of the century. It must therefore have been written after Paul's letters began to circulate.

The earlier date

Conservative scholars have argued for a date prior to the fall of Jerusalem.[63] J. A. T. Robinson (not a conservative scholar), in

---

[59] The "Blessing on the Heretics" which was really a curse, rather than a blessing. It read: "Let Nazarenes and minim (heretics) perish in a moment, let them be blotted out of the book of the living, and let them not be written with the righteous." It is generally held to have been introduced at the Council of Jamnia in AD 75.

[60] More details on this argument and the opinions of Dougles Hare and von Tilborg are discussed in footnote 45 above.

[61] Craig Keener, *Matthew*, p 42.

[62] Craig Keener, *Matthew*, p 43.

[63] Guthrie, p 53–56; F.F. Bruce, *The New Testament Documents: Are They Reliable?* London: IVP, 1972, p 12; Carson & Moo, p 152–156; Leon Morris, *The Gospel According to Matthew*, Leicester: Eerdmans,

his rather controversial *Redating the New Testament,* reversed the usual arguments based on the fall of Jerusalem and the synoptic records of Christ's prediction of this event. He argued that far from indicating a date after AD 70, these passages (Mark 13, Luke 27, Matthew 24) argue for a date prior to AD 70 for all three synoptic gospels.[64] He then gave further reasons for an earlier dating of Matthew. There are certain links between Paul and Matthew indicating that Paul may have known what he called the "proto-Matthean collection" (what we called Matthew 1 above). Robinson believed there are different stages or "layers" evident in Matthew. Some elements indicate that it is the earliest gospel and some that it is the latest synoptic gospel. Papias's statement, while not fitting the extant gospel, may therefore fit the earlier proto-Matthean collection. Matthew also has elements which indicate that the break with Judaism was not yet complete. The tension between church and synagogue was still acutely felt.[65] His interest in Sabbath laws (12.5–7), in sacrifice (9.13), his denunciation of the Sadducees (16.1–12) and his interest in the half-shekel tax (17.24–27) all argue for a date before the destruction of the temple, when all such issues would have become obsolete. Robinson therefore dated Matthew between AD 50 and 64.[66] There are also links between the concept of the *parousia* (Second Coming) in Paul's

1992, p 8–11; R. T. France, *Matthew,* p 82–91.

[64] J.A.T. Robinson, *Redating the New Testament,* p 13–30. Scholars who defend a later date tend not to take Robinson very seriously. However, those who defend the earlier date tend to make the point that his actual arguments have never really been answered in detail. One cannot circumvent an authors arguments by simply disparaging his work.

[65] This subject is covered in more detail in footnote 45 above.

[66] Robinson p 353.

letters to the Thessalonians and Matthew 24.[67] Then there are also indications that Luke may have known Matthew. If Acts is dated prior to Paul's trial in AD 64, and Luke is therefore earlier than that, the date of Matthew gets pushed back still earlier.[68]

Since the fall of Jerusalem is one of the only fixed dates at our disposal (other than the trial of Paul in AD 64 relative to the date of Acts), the language Matthew uses for this event is a fairly pivotal argument. Those who affirm a later date make much of how the language shows knowledge of this event. Yet such assumptions are quite subjective, for a number of reasons.[69]

1. For those who doubt the possibility of accurate prediction, which is of course a particular form of bias, there is the fact that any astute reader of the drift of Jewish-Roman politics at the time could have come to the conclusion that a clash was inevitable.[70]

2. Descriptive language for the destruction of the city and the temple was readily available from Old Testament references to similar events in the past, particularly in the Septuagint. Matthew's language need not reflect anything more than

---

[67] Robinson p 97–107.

[68] This argument is noted by Guthrie, p 55.

[69] This is described in the now famous comment by Bo Reicke as "an amazing example of uncritical dogmatism" in New Testament Scholarship, "Synoptic Prophecies on the Destruction of Jerusalem," in D. W. Aune, editor, *Studies in New Testament and Early Christian Literature: Essay in Honor of Allen P.Wikgren* (Novum Testamentum Suppl.33), Leiden: Brill, 1972, p 121–134.

[70] T. T. France, *Matthew* writes: "any reasonably acute observer of first-century Palestine must have seen that Jewish revolt and Roman reprisals were at least a possibility, and that if this were to happen the destruction of Jerusalem, and especially of the temple, would be likely" p 84–85.

knowledge of the Septuagint.[71]

3. In one item, Matthew's record of Jesus words runs counter to what actually happened. The disciples are told to "flee to the mountains" (24.16). When the Christians did flee, in AD 66, they went to Pella, which is not in the mountains.[72] Further, if Christians did flee the city prior to its fall, then there is evidence that Christ's predictions were known and followed at that time.

Some of the arguments for the later date do not make that much sense.

1. The idea that a high Christology is "late" cannot explain how Paul's letters have an equally high, or perhaps higher Christology and were all written well before any of the gospels.

2. Statements about "until today" can be just as relevant 30 years after events as much later. One has only to consider books written in our time about events that took place thirty years ago to recognize how silly this argument is.

3. Arguments about Paul's letters would have to apply equally to Mark, and many scholars date Mark before AD 70.

---

[71] R.T. France, *Matthew* writes: "The language of this verse, as of other gospel predictions of the fall of Jerusalem, draws both on the regular features of Roman warfare and on the standard terminology of accounts of punitive expeditions in the Old Testament and Jewish world", p 84.

[72] Guthrie, p 55.

Conclusion

As with authorship, the information available to us at present cannot conclusively argue either for the earlier or the later date. Further, it is possible to associate the later date with apostolic authorship, since someone who was a young man in AD 30 could still have been alive in AD 80. On balance however, the earlier date tends to support apostolic authorship more than the later date.

I favour the earlier dating. I believe arguments for a later dating of Luke-Acts are very difficult to support due to the fact that it is almost impossible to account for the fact that Luke, in Acts, does not seem to have any knowledge of the trail and martyrdom of Paul. I believe this factor more than counterbalances indications that Luke's language may show knowledge of the fall of Jerusalem. Since the language in all three synoptics that record Christ's predictions is fairly similar, I do agree with Robinson that it is better to date them all prior to the fall of Jerusalem.[73]

---

[73] I have dealt with the language used in Luke in more detail in *The Mission of the Kingdom: The Theology of Luke-Acts*, Vineyard International Publishing, 2011, and Amazon Kindle publication.

PLACE AND CONTEXT

More recent commentaries tend to place less weight on the issues of authorship and date than on the indications, from the gospel, of the social context in which it was written, and therefore who it was actually addressing.[74]

Place

While some scholars have suggested Alexandria, there are really only two viable contexts favoured by most scholars, either Palestine (or Galilee) or Syrian Antioch. Most prefer the latter. Some of the factors that support Antioch are:

- Matthew's gospel had an influence on Ignatius and the Didache. The former was based there, and the latter was probably written there.[75]
- Matthew "emphasizes locations in Syria (4.24), background that may fit only Syria (17.24–27), and advocates a Gentile mission that the Syrian Jewish church had first embraced."[76]
- Syria had the largest concentration of Jewish people outside

---

[74] An example would be Craig Keener, *Matthew.*
[75] Keener, *Matthew,* p 41.
[76] Keener, *Matthew,* p 41.

Palestine, especially Antioch.

- Luke records how Antioch became a major base for Christian mission. Due to its cosmopolitan population, but including a large Jewish community, it would be a more likely place for Christian theology, written in Greek, to arise than Jerusalem.
- Gundry's detailed work on Matthew's Old Testament quotations locates the author in a multilingual context (Greek, Aramaic and Hebrew). While a location in Palestine would fit this requirement, Antioch would qualify almost as well.

Matthew's intended audience

Older scholarsip tended to try to isolate particular communities as the context and audience of a given New Testament document. As knowledge of the social context of the ancient world has grown in recent years, this tendency has waned. As a generalization, it is now recognized that Judaism was more Hellenized than previously thought, and that Jews were more likely to be bilingual. The boundaries between cultures was more fluid than previously thought. For instance, it is now generally thought likely that Jesus would have been able to speak Greek, and perhaps read Greek.

Further it is unlikely that any author writing a text in Greek would have aimed it at a narrow audience located within one small community. Part of the reason to write in Greek was to be able to appeal to as wide an audience as possible. Further, since Matthew shows a strong interest in the mission to the Gentiles, one can assume that he wanted his text to be read as widely as possible.

To balance this however are indications that he did not feel it necessary to explain certain Jewish customs to his readers. So for instance when the Jewish leaders complain that the disciples of Jesus do not wash their hands properly, Matthew simply records what Jesus says with no explanation (15.1–10), whereas Mark adds a long explanation for his intended Gentile audience (Mark 7.3–4). Where Matthew and Mark describe the "abomination of desolation" with the added clause, "let the reader understand", Luke leaves this phrase out altogether, presumably because he knows it would not have been readily understood by a Gentile audience. Matthew leaves transliterated Aramaic words without explanation (*raka* – 5.22; *mamonas*/money – 6.24; *korbanas*/blood money – 27.6) and includes a number of Jewish customs unexplained (phylacteries and tassels – 23.5; burial customs – 23.27, Sabbath travel issues – 24.20).

These factors, together with the very Jewish characteristics of Matthew that we have already noticed (rabbinical literary style, midrashic typological reading of the Old Testament), together with the likely place of Syrian Antioch or somewhere in Palestine, together with the evidence that the break between church and synagogue was still in process, all combine to lead to the conclusion that Matthew was writing mainly to a Jewish Christian audience that may have included Gentiles, rather than to a predominantly Gentile Christian audience that may have included some Jews.

Yet even with this statement, one should not overdo the boundaries between these communities. For instance, if one examines the letter to the Hebrews, it becomes evident that the author was skilled in both Jewish midrashic interpretation and in Greek rhetoric and wrote to appeal to readers who would have been impressed by the use of both forms of literature or argument.[77]

Can one narrow down the context any further? Here the various suggestions tend to assume which date a given author has decided on. Those who date Matthew after AD 70 are more confident that his primary opponents where the rabbi's who rose to prominence after the war which ended in the fall of Jerusalem. Keener comments:

> Matthew's special target appears to be the successors of the scribes and Pharisees, the founders of the rabbinic movement at Jamnia and whatever Jewish leaders throughout Syro-Palestine may have been aligned with or influenced by them.[78]

However R. T. France, who favours an earlier dating, uses all the same rabbinical characteristics in Matthew to come to the conclusion that none of these features about Matthew's opponents need lead to a later date.[79]

As with authorship and date, the evidence available to us does not allow for a definitive answer as to the exact kind of Jewish Christian audience Matthew was writing to, be it pre or post AD 70.

For teaching

One characteristic almost all scholars are agreed on is that Matthew wrote to equip Church teachers and preachers. The way he lays out his material, in clear blocks of teaching, the way he uses sets of seven, or three, and the way he has sometimes abbrevi-

---

[77] See Derek Morphew, *The Prophets Voice, Hebrews: Prophecy, Rhetoric, Interpretation,* Amazon Kindle publication.

[78] Craig Keener, *Matthew,* p 46.

[79] R. T. France, *Matthew,* p 95–102

ated Mark to be able to include as many stories and teachings of Jesus as possible, within the available length of a standard manuscript at the time, all go to suggest that he was consciously writing some sort of teaching manual. And he was successful, because Matthew became by far the most used gospel in the church for centuries.

BIBLIOGRAPHY

E. L. Abel, "Who Wrote Matthew", *New Testament Studies,* 17, 1970–71, p 138–152.

W. F. Albright & C. S. Mann, *Matthew,* New York: Doubleday, 1971.

W. C. Allen, *The Gospel According to Saint Matthew,* ICC, Edinburgh: T. & T. Clark, 1922.

K. E. Bailey, "Informal Controlled Oral Tradition and the Synoptic Gospels," *Asia Journal of Theology* 5, 1991.

J. P. Brennan, "Virgin and Child in Isa.7.14", *Bible Today,* 1, 1964, p 968–971.

F. F. Bruce, *Commentary on the Epistle to the Hebrews, NICNT,* Grand Rapids: Eerdmans, 1964.

F. F. Bruce, *The New Testament Documents: Are They Reliable?* London: IVP, 1972.

Frederick Dale Bruner, *Matthew, A Commentary: The Christbook 1–12,* Grand Rapids: Eerdmans, 2004.

J. Edgar Bruns, "Matthew's Genealogy of Jesus," *Bible Today,* 6, 1964, p 980–985.

Günther Bornkamm, Heinz Joachim Held & Gerhard Barth, *Tradition and Interpretation in Matthew,* London: SCM, 1963.

Colin Brown, editor, *The New International Dictionary of New*

Testament Theology, Volume III, Exeter: Paternoster, 1975.

D.A. Carson & Douglas J. Moo, *An Introduction to the New Testament,* Grand Rapids: Zondervan, 1992.

Oscar Cullman, *The Christology of the New Testament,* London, SCM, 1971.

W. D. Davies, *The Setting of the Sermon on the Mount,* Cambridge: Cambridge University Press, 1963.

Charles T. Davis, "The fulfilment of Creation. A Study of Matthew's Genealogy", *Journal of American Academic Religion,* 41, 1973, p 520–535.

C. H. Dodd, *The Founder of Christianity,* London: Collins, 1970.

James Dunn, *Jesus Remembered. Christianity in the Making: Volume I,* Michigan: Eerdmans, 2003.

Floyd V. Filson, *The Gospel According to Saint Matthew,* London: Adam & Charles Black, 1960.

R. T. France, *Jesus and the Old Testament,* London: Tyndale, 1971.

R. T. France, *Matthew: Evangelist and Teacher,* Paternoster, 1992.

T. Francis Glasson, "Anti-Pharisaism in St. Matthew", *Jewish Quarterly Review,* 51, 1961, p 316–320.

M. D. Goulder, *Midrash and Lection in Matthew,* London: S.P.C.K.,1974.

Joel Green, *The Gospel of Luke,* NICNT, Grand Rapids: Eerdmans, 1997.

Robert H. Gundry, "The Language Milieu of First Century Palestine: It's Bearing on the Authenticity of the Gospel Tradition", *Journal of Biblical Literature,* 83, 1964, p 404–408.

Robert H. Gundry, *The Use of the Old Testament in St. Matthew's Gospel, With Special Reference to the Messianic Hope,* Leiden: E. J. Brill, 1975.

Donald Guthrie, *New Testament Introduction,* Leicester: IVP, 1990.

Douglas Hare, *The Theme of Jewish Persecution of Christians in the*

Gospel According to Matthew, London: Cambridge University Press, 1967.

Ralph W. Harris, editor, *Harmony of the Gospels,* Springfield: R.R. Donnelley & Sons, 1986.

David Hill, *Matthew, The New Century Bible,* London: Marshall, Morgan & Scott, 1972.

Martin Hengel, *Studies in the Gospel of Mark,* Philadelphia: Fortress Press, 1985.

William Hendriksen, *Matthew: New Testament Commentary,* Banner of Truth, 1973.

S. E. Johnson, *Matthew, The Interpreters Bible,* New York: Abingdon, 1951.

Leon Morris, *The Gospel According to Matthew,* Leicester: Eerdmans, 1992.

Craig Keener, *A Commentary on the Gospel of Matthew,* Grand Rapids: Eerdmans, 1999.

G. D. Kilpatrick, *The Origins of the Gospel According to Saint Matthew,* Oxford: Clarendon, 1946.

Jack Dean Kingsbury, *Matthew: Structure, Christology, Kingdom,* Philadelphia, Fortress, 1975.

Edgar Krentz, "The Extent of Matthew's Prologue. Toward the Structure of the First Gospel," *Journal of Biblical Literature,* 83, 1964, p 409–414.

W.G. Kümmel, *Introduction to the New Testament,* London: SCM, 1970.

Ralph P. Martin, "St. Matthew's Gospel in Recent Study," *Expository Times,* 80, 1969, p 132.

A. H. McNeil, *The Gospel According to St. Matthew,* New York: MacMillan, 1965.

Helen Milton, "The Structure of the Prologue to St. Matthew's Gospel", *Journal of Biblical Literature,* 81, 1962, p 175–181.

Derek Morphew, *A Critical Investigation of Infancy Narratives in the Gospels According to Matthew and Luke,* Doctoral Dissertation, University of Cape Town, 1980.

Derek Morphew, *Breakthrough: Discovering the Kingdom,* Vineyard International Publishing, 2006, and Amazon Kindle publication, 2011.

Derek Morphew, *The Mission of the Kingdom: The Theology of Luke-Acts,* Vineyard International Publishing, 2011, and Amazon Kindle publication.

Derek Morphew, *The Prophets Voice, Hebrews: Prophecy, Rhetoric, Interpretation,* Amazon Kindle publication, 2011.

Derek Morphew, *Biblical Interpretation 101,* Amazon Kindle publication, 2011.

R.E. Nixon, "Matthew", *New Bible Commentary,* London: IVP, 1967.

Norman Perrin, *The New Testament, an Introduction,* New York: Harcourt Brace Javonavich, 1974.

E. Stewart Petrie, "The Authorship of 'The Gospel According to Matthew', A Reconstruction of the External Evidence," *New Testament Studies,* 14, 1967–68, p 15–30.

Bo Reicke, "Synoptic Prophecies on the Destruction of Jerusalem," in D. W. Aune, editor, *Studies in New Testament and Early Christian Literature: Essay in Honor of Allen P.Wikgren* (Novum Testamentum Suppl.33), Leiden: Brill, 1972, p 121–134.

James A. T. Robinson, *Redating the New Testament,* London: SCM, 1976.

Krister Stendahl, *Matthew, Peake's Commentary on the Bible,* London: Nelsons, 1962.

Krister Stendahl, *The School of Saint Matthew and its Use of the Old Testament,* Philadelphia: Fortress, 1968.

Wilhelm Schneemelcher, *New Testament Apocrypha*, Philadelphia: Westminster John Knox Press, 2006.

Eduard Schweizer, "Observance of the Law and Charismatic Activity in Matthew", *New Testament Studies,* 16, p 67–70.

Frank Stagg, *Matthew, The Broadman Bible Commentary,* Volume 8, Nashville: Broadman Press,1969.

Sjef van Tilborg, *The Jewish Leaders in Matthew,* Leiden: E. J. Brill, 1972.

CPSIA information can be obtained at www.ICGtesting.com
Printed in the USA
LVOW10s0447161215

466789LV00020B/310/P